ADORNO: A C
THE PERP

ADORNO: A GUIDE FOR THE PERPLEXED

ALEX THOMSON

continuum
LONDON • NEW YORK

CONTINUUM
The Tower Building
11 York Road
London SE1 7NX

15 East 26th Street
New York
NY 10010

First published 2006
www.continuumbooks.com

© Alex Thomson 2006

British Library Cataloguing-in-Publication Data
A catalogue record for this book is available from the British Library.

ISBN: HB: 0–8264–7419–5
PB: 0–8264–7420–9

Library of Congress Cataloging-in-Publication Data
Thomson, A. J. P. (Alexander John Peter)
    Adorno: a guide for the perplexed / Alex Thomson.
       p.   cm. — (Guides for the perplexed)
    Includes bibliographical references and index.
    ISBN 0–8264–7419–5 (hardcover: alk. paper) —
ISBN 0–8264–7420–9 (pbk.: alk. paper)
    1. Adorno, Theodor W., 1903–1969.   I. Title.   II. Series.
B3199.A34T475 2006
193—dc22

2005021238

Typeset by Servis Filmsetting Ltd, Manchester
Printed and bound in Great Britain by MPG Books Ltd, Cornwall

CONTENTS

CONTENTS

ABBREVIATIONS

AE	*Against Epistemology: A Metacritique* trans. Willis Domingo, Oxford: Blackwell, 1982.
AP	'The Actuality of Philosophy', *Telos* 31 (1977): 120–33.
AT	*Aesthetic Theory* trans. Robert Hullot-Kentor, London: Athlone, 1992.
CI	*The Culture Industry: Selected Essays on Mass Culture* ed. J.M. Bernstein, London: Routledge, 1991.
CM	*Critical Models* trans. Henry Pickford, New York: Columbia University Press, 1998.
DE	*Dialectic of Enlightenment: Philosophical Fragments* with Max Horkheimer, trans. Edmund Jephcott, Stanford: Stanford University Press, 2002.
EOM	*Essays on Music* ed. Richard Leppert, Berkeley: University of California Press, 2002.
INH	'The Idea of Natural History', trans. Robert Hullot-Kentor, *Telos* 32 (1977): 111–24.
MCP	*Metaphysics: Concepts and Problems* trans. Edmund Jephcott, Cambridge: Polity, 2000.
MM	*Minima Moralia* trans. Edmund Jephcott, London: New Left Books, 1974.
ND	*Negative Dialectics* trans. E.B. Ashton, London: Routledge, 1973.
NL I, II	*Notes to Literature* vols. I & II trans. Shierry Weber Nicholsen, New York: Columbia University Press, 1991–92.
OPM	'On Popular Music', with the assistance of George Simpson, in EOM, pp. 437–69.

P	*Prisms* trans. Samuel and Shierry Weber, Cambridge, MA: MIT Press, 1981.
PMP	*Problems of Moral Philosophy* trans. Rodney Livingstone, Cambridge: Polity, 2000.
QF	*Quasi Una Fantasia: Essays in Modern Music* trans. Rodney Livingstone, London: Verso, 1992.
RS	'The Radio Symphony', trans. Susan H. Gillespie, in EOM, pp. 251–70.
TPC	'Theory of Pseudo Culture', trans. Deborah Cook, *Telos* 95 (1993): 15–38.

INTRODUCTION

Seldom do intellectual difficulties stem from mere lack of intelligibility; they are usually the result of shock.

(NL II 228–9)

The value of a thought is measured by its distance from the continuity of the familiar.

(MM 80)

The philosophical and critical works of Theodor Adorno (1903–69) are some of the most challenging produced in the twentieth century. Challenging in two senses of the word: in a weaker sense, that they present formidable difficulties of understanding and interpretation to the reader; and in a strong sense, that they seek to force us to rethink many things we take for granted, and to make us question the very possibility of philosophy, of art and of moral life in the contemporary world. Adorno's writing can often seem obscure, impenetrable and forbidding; doubly so for those with little knowledge of the philosophical traditions on which he draws. But more troubling is the way he often sets out to confound what we take for common sense, and to attack what he sees as the dominant trends in twentieth-century European and American culture, trends which have only intensified since his death. As a result, most readers experience a sense of resistance to reading Adorno, a jolt to the system which can be almost as physical as it is intellectual: if the first question raised by his texts is: 'what does he mean?', the second question will often be: 'can he really mean that?'

Adorno sometimes characterized this effect in terms of shock, a shock which he also associated with certain kinds of modern art,

1

particularly the work of the composer Arnold Schoenberg. But by shock, Adorno does not simply mean to *épater les bourgeois*, to scandalize a complacent public with obscenity, or violence, or immorality. Unlike his great intellectual inspiration Walter Benjamin, Adorno had little time for surrealism, which he saw as a celebration of irrationalism, just as he was suspicious of the revolutionary Marxist politics embraced by his friend. No, for Adorno shock is something which he associates with philosophy itself: the fundamental impulse of metaphysics to transform the world, by going beyond the immediate surface of things, by not being content with appearances, by striving to replace mere opinion with truth. In *Negative Dialectics*, the most systematic statement of his philosophical position, Adorno comments that 'the power of the status quo puts up the facades into which our consciousness crashes. It must seek to crash through them' (ND 17). A thought that would be worth having would have to be difficult. This fundamental and principled commitment to difficulty raises subsidiary problems, which have perplexed many of Adorno's readers. In this introduction I will discuss a number of these secondary difficulties, in order that we might focus on the essential difficulty which alone matters to Adorno.

So why bother with Adorno? Simply that he is one of the most profound thinkers of the twentieth century; and he is so precisely to the extent that his work is difficult, in raising questions which we would prefer to avoid. At the heart of his work lies a profound sense of ambivalence over the possibility of freedom in the contemporary world, and an interrogation of the promises made for our freedom by the western intellectual tradition since Kant: that freedom depends on the assertion of our autonomy as individuals; that freedom comes from our submission to – or our rebellion against – social norms; that freedom comes through aesthetic experience; that freedom comes through conformity to the moral law. But this is an ambivalence which spreads to touch on pretty much the entirety of Adorno's work: the key questions for whom are simply: Is art possible? Is freedom possible? Is philosophy possible? Although Adorno's responses may be unusual, he addresses concerns which have been at the heart of western intellectual life for the last three hundred years.

If I insist on this philosophical dimension of Adorno's work, it is partly because it has been consistently underrated. Adorno is often presented, by both his critics and admirers, as some species of sociologist. It is certainly true that the great attraction of Adorno's work is that his work is not abstract but precisely engaged with the smallest details of the world around us. But Adorno does not just set out to *describe* the world: as we have seen, he wishes to break open the world of appearances and show how things really are. But since any attempt to go beyond the way the world presents itself to us must always be a matter of speculation, Adorno can best be described as a philosopher, even though his work challenges or even perverts some deeply held philosophical assumptions. The specific difficulty this raises is that when Adorno sketches out what look like historical arguments, they must be understood as speculative rather than sociological.

For all his concern with the effects of capitalism on the ways we act and on the ways we think, Adorno's task is not simply that of cataloguing the deformation of reason under the impact of particular economic or historical transformations. That would be to presume in advance that we know what history is, or where economics begins and ends. Rather, Adorno tries to find ways to interrogate the incapacity of reason to account for the evident failings of social life, given that thinking historically or economically might be just as much a part of the problem as they are the solution. Impatient critics have seen this as contradictory: surely Adorno relies on reason to interrogate reason? But this criticism only makes sense if we know in advance what reason is: whereas for Adorno the power of thought is precisely that it can, and must, leave secure ground and head into uncharted waters. Without the necessary risk this involves, we surrender the possibility of anything other than dogmatic metaphysics: founding our understanding of the world in conformity with a particular set of beliefs. In this Adorno continues the tradition of Enlightenment thought which he also seeks to put into question. In *Negative Dialectics* he comments that 'thought as such, before all particular contents, is an act of negation, of resistance to that which is forced upon it' (ND 19). What is forced upon it are rigidified, frozen patterns of thinking. Resistance to dogma means opposition to religious forms of thought, even where those forms claim to have been fully secularized, and whether they depend on faith in God, in the laws of the free market, or the triumph of the proletariat owing to the immutable laws of history.

Failure to adequately distinguish the transcendental dimension of Adorno's work, closely connected to the near constant reference to Kant in his methodological writings, has been responsible for much misunderstanding. For example, Adorno has often been compared to the British tradition which runs from Matthew Arnold to F.R. Leavis to Raymond Williams, in which the alienation and exploitation evident in industrialized mass society is criticized from the standpoint of culture. Adorno might equally be said to compare society as it is with the claims made on its behalf by culture. But the others do not share his remorseless scepticism about the powers usually attributed to high culture: art, poetry, music, philosophy. Both our flawed societies and the arts which have claimed to resolve their problems must be criticized. So for all Adorno's passionate commitment to the potential of art and of philosophy to change the world, his work also entails an essential hesitation about that power.

Distinguishing the philosophical dimension of Adorno's work, which governs the way we need to read it, is made harder by the fact that many of his key strategies and much of his philosophical vocabulary refers to the work of Hegel, a philosopher who until recently remained deeply unfashionable in Britain and America (largely as a reaction to the enthusiasms of an earlier generation of British philosophers). A comment such as: 'dialectics is the self-consciousness of the objective context of delusion' (ND 417) will make little sense unless we bear in mind that Hegel's dialectic purports to be a speculative construction of the self-consciousness of the universe: philosophy in his sense was the total self-comprehension of the world from both an objective and a subjective viewpoint. Adorno inverts this idea: dialectics does not deliver us the truth of the world, but rather knowledge of its untruth. In *Minima Moralia*, 'whose method' Adorno remarks was 'schooled' by that of Hegel, he writes: 'the whole is the false' (MM 16, 50). The title of *Negative Dialectics* itself should tell us that to understand Adorno's work we need to understand the claims made by Hegel, and why these are so compelling to Adorno, as well as why they need to be modified or revised. But the title of one of Adorno's idiosyncratic essays on Hegel, 'Skoteinos', a Greek word meaning darkness or obscurity, should be enough to warn us that this may not make things any easier.

Having said all this, we should bear in mind Adorno's comment in *Negative Dialectics*: 'Philosophy is the most serious of things; but then again it is not all that serious' (ND 14). Indeed, Adorno's entire attitude to philosophy is sceptical and critical. His work consists less in building up systems than in knocking them down. In this demolition project his inspiration is Nietzsche, one of the most notorious and iconoclastic figures of the late nineteenth century, as a passing comment made by Adorno in his 1965 lecture course on moral philosophy reveals: 'of all the so-called great philosophers I owe him by far the greatest debt – more even than to Hegel' (PMP 172). Of particular interest to us in preparing to read Adorno is the extent to which he takes over Nietzsche's conception of philosophy as a double task of destruction and creation. Adorno's revised understanding of dialectics means allowing philosophical and cultural alternatives to destroy each other: for example, by showing the complicity of knowledge with power, of morality with violence, of historical progress with the destruction of the natural world. By taking to its extreme the logic he sees as evident within the ways we generally think, Adorno seeks to unsettle us, and leave us without a certain ground on which to base our moral judgements. He believes that our desires for certainty, for absolutes, for fixed foundations or for security, are themselves violent and destructive forces which need to be challenged. In this Adorno is closer to pragmatism than to a thorough-going rationalism: his thinking is experimental, which means risking failure, but is a necessary condition of any possible progress: 'In principle philosophy can always go astray, which is the sole reason it can go forward' (ND 14).

Part of the experimental aspects of Adorno's writing is the unusual form of his work. Unlike many philosophers who work in the English language, Adorno does not see an absolute distinction between the content of a philosophical text and the manner of its presentation. The shock value of Adorno's work, which determines its critical potential, stems in part from his sense that the individual moments of an argument cannot be unfolded from a simple beginning, nor should they be subordinated to its conclusion. The essay is the most characteristic vehicle of Adorno's work, and we need to remember that 'essay' also means something experimental, an attempt. Adorno often refuses to define his terms, and arranges his material in such a way that there is often no clear hierarchy available between the various statements. Like an art work, the essay is defined by the 'reciprocal interaction' between the whole and its parts: 'the specific moments are not to be derived from the whole, nor vice versa' (NL I 14). The philosopher should not pretend to be able to provide a clear and rational explanation of the world, since the attempt to impose such patterns on the world is bound up with man's violent domination of nature. Adorno's interest in dialectics means that he sees identity as relational. Concepts are not clearly distinct logical entities, but mobile and slippery frames for apprehending reality, whose interactions are always evolving. Rather than seek to freeze this movement, the form of the essay should try to imitate it.

This undoubtedly means hard work for every reader of Adorno, however familiar they are with the general outline of his thought. His work needs to be read with the same care with which we would listen to complex music. Adorno himself compares reading Hegel to listening to a Beethoven symphony, and these comments are one of the best guides to how to read his own texts:

> Highly organized music too must be heard multidimensionally, forward and backward at the same time. Its temporal organizing principle requires this: time can be articulated only through distinctions between what is familiar and what is not yet familiar, between what already exists and what is new; the condition of moving forward is a retrogressive consciousness. One has to know a whole movement and be aware retrospectively of what has come before. The individual passages have to be grasped as consequences of what has come before, the meaning of a divergent repetition has to be evaluated, and reappearance has to be perceived not merely as architectonic correspondence but as something that has evolved with necessity.[1]

All of Adorno's works demand patient and sympathetic reading, which seeks to press beyond any initial shock to examine their overall coherence and structure. But we must also remember that he believes that the confidence of Beethoven or Hegel in the ultimate resolution of the parts within the harmonious totality of the work is no longer possible. So what we are really looking for is the way his work gestures to a coherence which it must also fail to achieve. This deliberate failure to resolve is an attempt to keep faith with the resistance of the world to objectifying thought. Adorno's favourite motif to characterize his approach is that of the constellation:

> [The essay's] concepts are to be presented in such a way that they support one another, that each becomes articulated through its configuration with the others. In the essay discrete elements set off against each other come together to form a readable context; the essay erects no scaffolding and no structure. But the elements

6

crystallize as a configuration through their motion. The constellation is a force field, just as every intellectual structure is necessarily transformed into a force field under the essay's gaze. (NL I 13)

Adorno's essays do not necessarily proceed from basic premises to clear conclusions: they are more playful, seeking to explore the ways concepts interact with each other from different angles. Often this can seem repetitive, as the same point is taken up again and again, but in a different light each time.

As a result of his ambitious objectives, of their range of reference, and of the fact that the form and style of his work is part and parcel of its power, Adorno's texts place exceptional demands on their readers. While it is often obvious which positions Adorno does not agree with, he rarely makes a positive conclusion explicit: if the burden of decision were to be taken off the reader, he would be betraying the Enlightenment principle that freedom comes through the free and autonomous use of reason. The aim of this book is to make it easier to read Adorno: but in doing so it risks betraying that premise of his work. Consequently, it cannot be intended to *replace* a reading of Adorno's work, but to precede and accompany it. Getting to know the work of a philosopher is not like buying a piece of flat-pack furniture and this *Guide for the Perplexed* cannot be a simple instruction book. Even in his own lifetime Adorno faced the challenge of continually testing his own theory against evolving historical circumstances. His readers must do the same: there can be no question of taking it up as an off-the-shelf solution. The specific historical configuration in which Adorno's ideas took shape may well have passed; but so long as the philosophical ailments for which Adorno's work offers treatment remain dominant his work will be not only of relevance but of great importance. To understand Adorno in English rather than German, at a point in time at which both the political and philosophical upheavals of the twentieth century may seem *passé*, out of date, lingering spectres, requires a complex gesture of translation. Adorno must be brought towards us; but we must reach out to Adorno too. The intransigence of these problems should not be underestimated, and we should certainly be suspicious of assuming or seeking a casual familiarity with Adorno's thought: when we are no longer perplexed by his work, we are no longer reading; we are no longer thinking. How we are to read Adorno must remain a problem.

For many commentators on Adorno such difficulties are so great that they cannot be overcome; or perhaps they do not judge the results worth the effort. I do not believe this is true or I could not have even begun to write this book, which has also of course been part of my own struggle to come to terms with Adorno. The historian of Marxism Leszek Kolakowski prefaces his discussion of *Negative Dialectics* with the claim that 'the pretentious obscurity of style and the contempt that it shows for the reader might be endurable if the book were not also totally devoid of literary form'; Martin Jay begins the only other short introductory book in English on Adorno's work by arguing that his subject 'would have been appalled at a book of this kind dedicated to him' and 'would have had a principled objection to any attempt to render his thought painlessly accessible to a wide audience'.[2] But Adorno's style is designed to challenge, perhaps even to provoke: since any allergic responses must be automatic, a matter of instinct, overcoming our own shock must be the necessary condition of a free response. There is no question of contempt for the reader; nor does Adorno believe in anything other than engagement with the widest possible audience. What he does not believe is that one should pander to an audience by presenting work in forms which betray its fundamental principles, or by flattering them that they will find the work easy. This is not because he judges his audience incapable of understanding, but because he continues to imagine, despite all the evidence, that human beings are rational creatures capable of overcoming their own resistance to thought. In this, Adorno remains a philosopher, even as he probes the moral and epistemological limits of rational knowledge of reality, and thus brings philosophy itself into question.

In *Adorno: A Guide for the Perplexed* I have chosen to focus on three aspects of his thought: his work on art and culture; the relationship between his social and moral thought, organized around the problem of freedom; and the interaction between philosophy and history. Each of these is dealt with in a single chapter, which might be read on its own, although there are many cross-connections between them, and a relatively sophisticated picture of Adorno will only emerge from bearing all three in mind at once. Because of the difficulty of Adorno's thought I have added a preliminary chapter in which I provide some background information on Adorno's life and times, and sketch out what I see as the primary political motivation of his work. On the basis of such an outline I believe it is much easier to see what is distinctive about Adorno's work, and particularly his insistence on the categories of mediation, dialectics and negativity. For all their philosophical weight, such terms in Adorno's work are deployed as strategic responses to particular configurations of historical forces; indeed at points the strain shows as the terms are subjected to greater loads than they may reasonably bear.

However much he admired his friend's work, Benjamin, Adorno suggests, remains at heart a *believer*: there are traces of a slightly naïve faith in a better future – what Adorno calls an 'undialectical positivity' – equally present in both his early and later thought, despite his apparent shift from a religious to a Marxist point of view (ND 17). What Adorno offers instead, attributing it to his idiosyncratic reading of Hegel, is an absolute insistence on negativity, on a relentlessly critical stance, an opposition not only to the world as it is today but to all ameliorative programmes and proposed alternatives. The real difficulty of Adorno's work is to read it in such a way that this negativity can be made to surrender its own utopian content, but without forfeiting its critical potential. For Benjamin, God or politics will save the day; for Adorno, only the painful struggle of every individual who is capable of it to overcome their own prejudices and habits of mind. As he puts it in conclusion to his essay 'Opinion Delusion Society' (three words that are almost synonymous for Adorno): 'Critical thought alone, not thought's complacent agreement with itself, may help bring about change' (CM 122).

CHAPTER 1

AGAINST AUTHENTICITY

'It is even part of my good fortune not to be a house-owner', Nietzsche already wrote in the Gay Science. *Today we should have to add: it is part of morality not to be at home in one's home.*

(MM 39)

'Philosophy is really homesickness,' says Novalis, 'it is the urge to be at home everywhere.'[1]

'Paradoxical, ironic, mercilessly critical,' writes Edward Said, 'Adorno was the quintessential intellectual, hating all systems, whether on our side or theirs, with equal distaste.'[2] There is certainly some truth in what was rapidly becoming a cliché by the time Said raised it in his 1993 radio lectures for the BBC. What most characterizes the writing of Theodor W. Adorno is exile: from the reassurance and familiarity of home and family; from mother tongue and from fatherland; from political or philosophical movements and schools. That Said discusses Adorno several times in his work suggests a partial identification with him, based on their shared love of music, but also on their common identity as exiles. There is a crucial difference, however. As a Palestinian whose wealthy family chose to have him educated in English-speaking schools and then the United States, Said found himself displaced through decisions made on his behalf. But Adorno's exile was self-imposed. He had made himself an intellectual exile even before the rise of the Nazi regime in the 1930s forced this musician, critic and philosopher, from an assimilated Jewish background and with Marxist leanings, to leave for Oxford and then the United States.

Adorno's later work is undoubtedly stamped by the years of physical displacement in which his critical models, style and agenda were
hardened. But the key to understanding Adorno is his sense that the
role of the intellectual, a relentless negativity which consists in
setting oneself against just about everything, is not either reaction
or response to geographical, political or historical upheaval, but
something more like a moral imperative, whose force Adorno had
felt long before he was ever physically required to leave his native
land. To turn against all that one thinks one knows, to question
everything, is the very condition of intellectual responsibility. Such
a task is not easy; it cannot be easy; it must not be easy. As soon as
thought comes to rest in self-assurance, in orthodoxy, in fidelity to
some code or programme, it betrays not only its own possible
freedom, but that of the whole world. This is the underlying challenge of Adorno's work.

But if we see Adorno only as an exile, we neglect the most uncanny
and disturbing sides of his thought. Adorno is above all a dialectical
thinker. In his hands the idea of dialectic will become a critical instrument of unparalleled conceptual power: and its most important
characteristic will be that of rebounding back on its starting point,
undercutting or unsettling the assumptions from which we began. So
rather than getting comfortable with the idea of Adorno's intellectual displacement, we should turn it inside out. The sense of exile has
a problematic correspondence with our attachment to home. So for
all the pathos and drama of the idea of the intellectual exile it may
be no surprise to find in Adorno a curious domesticity, a naïve and
ingenuous attachment to the comforts of the familiar, wherever he
happens to be geographically and culturally. The price of the intellectual's critical vantage point on society may be some degree of dis-
connection from everyday life, but we are deluding ourselves if we
think that such a perspective does not remain deeply embedded in the
assumptions and practices from which it claims to have freed itself.
In his work, Adorno did more than almost any other writer to
acknowledge this dilemma, the impossibility of opposition as well as
its absolute necessity.

In this preliminary chapter I will give an overview of Adorno's life
and work which seeks to give an idea of this dialectic: for the young
man, the fashionable pose of homelessness belied by the security of
his upbringing; for the émigré thinker in the USA, an uncanny sense
of recognition which undermines his supposed exile; a political and

physical return to Europe which is equally a new displacement; and an intellectual legacy characterized by the inability to fix and locate a thought whose every effort was directed to resisting the petrifaction of hasty categorization. But at each stage we need to observe a common theme, which I take to be the central political thrust of Adorno's work: an opposition to the notion of authenticity, to the idea that life or thought could somehow come home, that some programme or ideology, whether religious, social or personal, could end the alienation of man so commonly diagnosed by twentieth-century intellectuals. If for Adorno we live in a fallen world, only by the resolute refusal to deny ourselves comforts and compromises, even the slightest promise of reconciliation, may we avoid contributing not only to our own imprisonment but that of others. If this seems grim, we should remember to look at it from the other direction at the same time: dialectically. If there is no end to alienation, perhaps the diagnosis of alienation is itself the problem rather than a step towards a solution. Do the critics of the modern world find or invent the problems they claim to solve?

WEIMAR YEARS

Recalling Adorno's initial reluctance to leave Germany after the Nazi seizure of power, Leo Lowenthal attributes it to his friend's comfortable upper-middle-class background: 'it was an existence you just had to love if you were not dying of jealousy of this protected beautiful life where Adorno had gained the confidence which never left him'. Lowenthal, who remained on cordial terms with Adorno until the latter's death, remembered him as possessing a combination of both absolute self-confidence and a kind of naïvety: 'he just could not believe that to him, son of Oskar Wiesengrund, nephew of aunt Agathe, and son of Marie, anything might ever happen'.[3] Adorno was the son of a wealthy wine-merchant, Oskar Wiesengrund, but as Lowenthal intimates, the main presence in his early life was his mother Maria Calvelli-Adorno, whose last name he was to adopt later in life, and her sister Agathe, who also lived with the family. Adorno's childhood seems to have been happy, tranquil and pampered. He never lost his taste for small luxuries, and his later essays often include reminiscences of childhood incidents or fancies – a trip to the zoo, the visit of an exotic-seeming relative, the child lying awake listening to the sound of music coming from the parlour. The critic of music, he suggests in a very early piece (1929), should moderate the nit-picking of the expert with something of the naïvety of the child: 'to think about twelve-tone technique at the same time as remembering that childhood experience of *Madama Butterfly* on the gramophone – that is the task facing every serious attempt to understand music today' (QF 20). Indeed a positive notion of childhood play, as a purposeless activity at odds with the rational and productive enterprises which are supposed to dominate adult life, runs like a subterranean current through all of Adorno's work.

It has often been remarked that the man retained something childlike in his character. Jürgen Habermas notes that 'in the presence of "Teddy" one could play out in an uncircumspect way the role of "proper" adult, because he was never in a position to appropriate for himself that role's strategies of immunization and adaptation. In every institutional setting he was "out of place", and not as if he intended to be.'[4] These anecdotal reminiscences of the man have serious consequences for how we might read the work. Robert Hullot-Kentor argues that what has appeared to many as Adorno's pessimism is really the critical counterpart of a 'naïve optimism': his colleagues were often puzzled by the apparent contrast between the 'intense seriousness' of the work and the man himself, who could often be not merely jolly but even whimsical or, as Hullot-Kentor puts it, 'silly'.[5] Adorno's total self-belief, which led the wife of his friend and collaborator Max Horkheimer to describe him as the 'most immense narcissist to be found in the Old and the New World', a charge which he himself conceded in part (QF 269), lent him a kind of brutal honesty in his intellectual dealings which has been described as 'owlishly egocentric – in the sense of an owl who lets no hushed mouse creep past him at night, though in the light of day is almost blind'.[6] Willing to risk friendships on fine points of intellectual principle, Adorno could also be clumsily, almost embarrassingly, effusive in his dealings with those he admired, such as the novelist Thomas Mann, or his great musical hero Schoenberg. It is tempting to ascribe this confidence, the basis from which he could maintain his endlessly confrontational and critical intellectual stance, to the unquenchable optimism of the spoilt child. A critic of Adorno dismisses him as 'secure in his self-centred aesthetic Marxism': the diagnosis seems partly fair.[7] The shelter of his early life seems to have provided Adorno with an unshakeable sense of security, and the ability to make himself at home wherever he found himself.

So when the young Adorno and his friend Siegfried Kracauer joke in letters to Lowenthal that they are agents of an organization for the 'Transcendentally Homeless' one of them at least is striking a pose.[8] Adorno's homelessness was figurative rather than literal, the expression of an adolescent sensibility shaped in the murky turn-of-the-century backwash of the tide of European Romanticism. Fifteen at the close of the 1914–18 war, Adorno reached a precocious intellectual maturity, entering university a year early at 17, pursued his musical and philosophical studies, and began his career as writer and academic in the Germany of the Weimar era (1918–33). Beyond the very real political and economic instability of these years, many artists and writers of the time shared a common perception of a crisis of spiritual values. The creative tumult of the period was dominated by an apocalyptic sense of decay and the concomitant need for a renewal, not so much of institutions, but of mankind itself. Amidst what the historian Friedriche Meinecke described in 1924 as a widespread and powerful sense of 'deep yearning for the inner unity and harmony of all laws of life and events in life', many young intellectuals saw the world as purposeless and barren, often shuttling between nostalgic invocations of an imagined sense of community and messianic hopes for the future, between mourning lost traditions and seeking to shatter what remained of them, between total political disengagement and extremist politics.[9] The idea of a transcendental homelessness with which Adorno and Kracauer are flirting comes from Georg Lukács's *Theory of the Novel* (1920). Subsequently repudiated by its author in his orthodox Marxist phase, this book was an enduring influence on more heretical adherents of the cause like Adorno. The phrase suggests existence in a world in which meaning is not immediately apparent, but in which the individual is confronted by forbidding and incomprehensible surfaces. Lukács describes this condition as a world of second nature: what appears to us as the natural conditions of our existence are in fact historical – they have appeared over time and as a consequence of the labour of man. For Lukács, we are adrift in a manmade world of second nature, and our task is to find our way home.

In later years Adorno recognized an affinity between the vocabulary of homelessness and what he called the 'jargon of authenticity', a pathos-laden tone of metaphysical grandeur which served to dramatize the essentially conservative cultural pronouncements of its users, however grounded in real needs their observations might be.[10]

With hindsight, the idea of homelessness seemed inextricably bound up with the fascist invocation of *Heimat* (homeland). Indeed the same comments from Novalis linking philosophy and homesickness that Lukács had cited in *Theory of the Novel* were to be invoked by Martin Heidegger in his 1929–30 lecture course on the problems of metaphysics; three years later he accepted the rectorship of Freiburg University from the Nazis. Whatever our evaluation of the relationship between Heidegger's political commitments and his philosophical work (Adorno could be almost hysterical on the subject, referring to Heidegger's thought as 'fascist right down to its innermost components'[11]), it is clear that this must be a troubling convergence. The relationship between Adorno and Heidegger has become central to recent philosophical re-evaluations of his work, particularly in English-language works, where the political stakes of establishing an absolute distinction between the two are lower than in Germany. But Adorno is certainly more aware than Heidegger not only of the political ambiguity of the idea of homelessness, but that the vocabulary of philosophy cannot easily be isolated from its political connotations. Adorno would never claim to be at home in the world. Such a gesture would imply the possibility of reconciliation, and substitute a concession to the status quo for the critical stance of the intellectual. While insisting on the possibility of progressive change, he goes to great lengths to avoid dramatizing such a change in terms of a homecoming or a return. This suspicion of any philosophical claim to be able to complete an 'inauthentic' everyday existence, alongside a scepticism towards systems and theories which claim to explain everything, is of central importance to his work.

This is a crucial point. The popularity of Ferdinand Tonnies' *Gemeinschaft und Gesellschaft* is revealing. Tonnies work was written in 1887, but after 1918 'rural nostalgia turned it into a best-seller, going through five more editions between 1920 and 1926'.[12] The title in translation is *Community and Society*, which gives some idea of the argument of the book, which inaugurates a tradition of sociological thinking in which some more 'natural' way of life – in Tonnies' case explicitly based on a quaint idea of medieval Germany – is contrasted with modern society. This opposition owes a great deal to Romantic historicism: a reaction against trends in modern development combined with a nostalgic or backwards-looking attitude, which tends to locate an absent source of value safely in the past. The reactionary temptation to dismiss the modern world is a tendency which runs deeply in twentieth-century western thought and culture. Indeed, many of Adorno's criticisms of modern society are familiar to us through the opposition of culture to commercial civilization found in the Victorian social commentary of Matthew Arnold, the criticism of T.S. Eliot, and in the work of F.R. Leavis and other writers connected to the journal *Scrutiny*, just as much as in the Marxist tradition – the work of Raymond Williams indicating the convergence of the two. But the influence of these ideas in psychological and sociological thought is equally widespread, and the idea of the modern world as somehow degenerate, and modern man as alienated, is a common one. It is worth specifying what makes Adorno's approach distinctive.

To do so we need to think about the grounds on which we might criticize modern society. As for Tonnies so for many cultural critics the standard by which the world in which we live is condemned is either historical, or utopian. Either we compare the modern world to that of the past, or some vision of future. To judge it against an older, and seemingly more fruitful, mode of existence is to run the risk of creating a retrospective fantasy. The utopian critique, which imagines how the world might look were some kind of rational plan for its improvement to be successfully implemented, must equally be a prisoner of its own times: it is a vision which depends on, and must reflect, the cultural assumptions of its own world. In his essay 'Cultural Criticism and Society' Adorno makes clear his opposition to what he describes as 'transcendental critique': because the cultural critic is always within the situation they describe, such criticisms are transcendental in claiming to have knowledge of another world beyond our own, whether an actual historical realm or a potential future, against which ours might be judged. The alternative he considers is immanent critique: this would mean judging the world not from some external viewpoint, but against the promises culture itself has made about the possible transformation and improvement of the world. The critic of culture 'is necessarily of the same essence as that to which he fancies himself superior', and so cannot claim to speak 'as if he represented either unadulterated nature or a higher historical stage'. This is an early lesson in Adorno's notion of dialectics: 'the subject itself is mediated down to its innermost make-up by the notion to which it opposes itself as independent and sovereign' (P 19).

This idea of mediation expressly contravenes the temptation to look for a more 'natural' or authentic existence. The collaborative textbook on *Aspects of Sociology* published by the Frankfurt School insists:

> As soon as thought concerning the social loses sight of the tension between that which is institutional and that which is living, as soon as, for instance, it no longer aids in the liberation from the compulsion of the institutions, but only furthers a new mythology, the glorification of illusory primal qualities, to which is attributed what in fact only arises by virtue of society's institutions. The extreme model of rendering society 'natural' in such a false and ideological fashion is the racist insanity of National Socialism. The *praxis* which was linked to these racist theories has shown that the Romantic critique of institutions, once it has broken out of the dialectics of society, is transformed into the dissolution of all protective and humane guarantees, into chaos, and ultimately, into rendering the institutions naked absolutes, pure dominating force.[13]

There are many similar passages in Adorno's writing: crucially, they underline the insufficiency of a historical or sociological approach to the problem. This is why Adorno rarely uses the idea of 'modernity': as soon as we define modern society in relation to a traditional or pre-modern social world, we risk reinventing some myth of man's prior natural existence. The dilemma Adorno faces is how to maintain a critical stance against the modern world when he accepts that there can be no sound appeal to a more authentic mode of existence. Whereas Lukács still believes in the possibility of first nature, for Adorno that must always remain a myth for those caught in second nature.

If the mature Adorno can still be usefully described as homeless, we must not imagine that he believes he can return home. So perhaps we should stress instead the 'transcendental' side of the phrase that the young Adorno borrows from *Theory of the Novel*. After all, his friendship with Kracauer, more than ten years his senior, began when the latter took on the role of providing the precocious youth with extracurricular philosophical studies, reading Immanuel Kant's *Critique of Pure Reason* together on Saturday afternoons. German universities of the time were dominated by Kantianism in various forms, so Adorno's early grounding in his work is hardly surprising, but as he acknowledges in his tribute to

Kracauer, the older man's approach to the interweaving of history and philosophy was to have a lasting impact on his pupil: Kant became 'not mere epistemology' but 'a kind of coded text from which the historical situation of spirit could be read' (NL II 58). The prevailing neo-Kantianism of the era saw philosophy as dealing with a set of methodological questions about the limits of knowledge quite distinct from any historical considerations, which were to be left to the other disciplines in the humanities, just as knowledge of the natural world was the proper concern of the natural sciences.

Adorno's fundamental conception of the task of philosophy, and of the inadequacy of sociological or historical attempts to resolve the dilemmas of existence, is decisively shaped by his encounter with Kant. In particular it determines the relationship between empirical and transcendental knowledge in his work. Kant's opposition to metaphysics is matched by Adorno's mistrust of any argument which assumes that 'truth' or 'value' may be found in another realm of existence; but Kant's insistence that knowledge cannot be based on empirical grounds rules out any simple appeal to the way things are. Our idea of what the facts of the matter really are will always depend on prior assumptions about what a fact is: these concepts are more than mere facts, abstractions from experience, but are not timeless transcendental categories. Rather, for Kant, as Adorno argues in his lectures on the *Critique of Pure Reason*, they exist in a kind of no-man's land.[14] This notion illuminates Adorno's own use of both concepts and historical arguments: he is never making direct statements about the way the world is, but exploring the concepts and arguments which claim to tell us about reality. By showing that these concepts and arguments can never quite match up to the world, he affirms the existence of the world (Adorno is a realist in this sense) as that which resists conceptual appropriation. This sense of thought as forever failing to catch up with the reality it seeks to describe is typical of Romantic and late nineteenth-century vitalist thinking, and is particularly strong in Nietzsche. As a way of making sense of 'transcendental homelessness' it also underlines the restlessness of the dialectic: the ceaseless struggle of thinking, which depends on concepts, to comprehend the world, which is non-conceptual.

Kracauer's insistence that Kant's writings might be read not as mere workbooks for a new logic but as the expression of competing historical and intellectual forces can be seen as preparing the way for

Adorno's interest in Lukács, who equally insisted on the interrelationship of philosophy and history. For the Lukács of *History and Class Consciousness* (1920) it was the recovery of the Hegelian roots of Marxism which would provide the requisite theoretical grounding for a view of the world as a whole, rather than the partial perspectives fostered by neo-Kantian thinking; but Adorno, coming under the influence of more anarchic works with strong theological elements to them, such as Ernst Bloch's *Spirit of Utopia*, and in particular the writings of Walter Benjamin, whose *The Origins of German Tragic Drama* (1928) was as important to him as his close friendship with its author, took a different path. It was with Benjamin as catalyst that Adorno's first major philosophical texts were written: lectures on 'The Language of Philosophy' (1930), 'The Actuality of Philosophy' (1931), 'The Idea of Natural History' (1932), and a monograph *Kierkegaard: Construction of the Aesthetic*, published inauspiciously on 27 February 1933, the day Hitler came to power in Germany. Adorno's vocabulary and approach in these early works is deeply indebted to Benjamin, who seems to have provided the theoretical tools with which Adorno could outline his own positions.

That Adorno should become a philosopher was by no means inevitable: he had been writing and publishing essays and reviews on music since he had left university in 1924, and could have continued his career as a journalist; and after spending time in Vienna studying with Alban Berg in 1925, it had seemed as if he might pursue a career as a composer. As it was, the experience of close involvement with the artistic circle around Berg would stay with Adorno throughout his life, and as both an accomplished composer and a philosopher he was later able to write about aesthetics as much from the point of view of the artist as from that of the theorist. But while continuing to compose, and also working as an editor and music critic, Adorno returned to philosophy. Supported by his father's money, and after some false starts, he succeeded in having the Kierkegaard study accepted for the *Habilitation*, the examination which would qualify him as a university lecturer. He joined the University of Frankfurt in 1931, the same year in which Horkheimer, with whom he had been friends for some years, became head of the Institute for Social Research. Established in 1924, the institute was openly Marxist, and mainly devoted to the history of the socialist movements; under Horkheimer's direction the institute was to change direction, combining economic and historical analyses with work in social theory and philosophy. But if Adorno hoped that his position at the university would mean the establishment of a new intellectual home, where personal, political and intellectual commitments might be united, he was to be mistaken. The Nazi government rapidly moved to imple ment its anti-Semitic policies, and like many other scholars with university positions, he lost his right to teach in September 1933. As the intellectual migration from Germany began in the face of rising violence and the persecution of Jews and suspected socialists, Adorno left for Oxford to continue his philosophical studies in 1934.

IN AMERICA

In 1938, Adorno arrived in New York, ostensibly to work on the Princeton Radio Project, an appointment arranged for him by Horkheimer, who remained director of the Institute for Social Research, which was now attached to Columbia University. The last four years had been spent working on a critical study of the phenomenology of Husserl in Oxford, punctuated by perilous trips back to Germany in order to see friends, collect money and to maintain his citizenship, and the chance for Adorno to settle in America was an attractive one. Horkheimer hoped that the connection to the prestigious project would prove valuable to the institute; it also meant having his friend Adorno in New York with him, without the expense of taking him on as a full-time member of the institute's staff. Paul Lazarsfeld, pioneer of empirical social research and director of the Princeton project, hoped for a productive and stimulating working relationship with a leading exponent of what he refers to in a letter to Adorno as the 'European approach'. By this he means 'a more theoretical attitude toward the research problem, and a more pessimistic attitude toward an instrument of technical progress'.[15] Having read at least Adorno's 'On the Social Situation of Music' (1932) in the journal of the institute, Lazarsfeld seems to have been aware of what he was getting. And Adorno? Looking back on his experience in an essay first given as a radio talk a number of years later, he accepts his 'naiveté about the American situation' (CM 217), by which he means both the cultural world of the USA, but also the specific working environment of the Princeton project. The working practices of empirical social research were 'utterly unfamiliar' to him (CM 219). Although Adorno's reminiscences should always be read with some care, since he often strikes particular poses to make a point, there is no reason in this instance to doubt that he had little idea of what he was in for.

These were years of bitterness and misunderstanding among the intelligentsia in exile, as they competed for the few financial resources available to support them in their host country; as Adorno notes in *Minima Moralia*, written at this time, 'relations between outcasts are even more poisoned then between long-standing residents' (MM 33). Ernst Bloch, for example, seems to have been resentful of Adorno's financial security, leading to an awkward incident when Adorno took seriously and publicized more widely what had been a slight exaggeration on Bloch's part in a letter asking for assistance: he was not in fact working as a dishwasher. Horkheimer found himself having to reconcile the numerous petitions for money from the Institute with the need to marshal resources for a stay of unknown duration. But the awkwardness was more pronounced in relations between the Germans and their hosts. Andrew Rubin has documented the bewilderment of FBI director J. Edgar Hoover when surveillance of the suspicious émigré group revealed telegrams between Adorno and Horkheimer apparently written in an obscure code revolving around such terms as 'Nietzsche' and 'Expressionism'.[16] But if the Americans found Adorno's culture alien, he found theirs depressing and restricted: in his colleagues on the radio project Adorno diagnosed a deep distrust of the kind of culture for which he had an unaffected appreciation. The suspicion was mutual: an American colleague described him subsequently as 'the most arrogant, self-indulgent (intellectually and culturally) man I have ever met'.[17]

Commentary on Adorno's time in America has tended to stress its negative aspects: the alien culture, the unfamiliarity of his new surroundings. Certainly, an unwillingness to compromise is the hallmark of those works produced in this period. Even before his arrival Horkheimer was warning Adorno of the need to adapt to his new environment; Lazarsfeld, responding to a lengthy provisional treatment of the problem sent from London, was reminding him of the fact that his project needed to produce concrete results, and that actual research could not be suspended indefinitely until a satisfactory theoretical model had been established. But, although he tried to adjust to more empirical research methods, a failure to produce results in the area of the project of which he was director led to the cancellation of that study in 1941. Whereas the Institute for Social

Research itself was funded out of the legacy of its major benefactor, Lazarsfeld's study was dependent on grants from the Rockefeller Foundation. Adorno found it hard to produce what in the deadening jargon of managerial academia would now be called 'research outputs'. With the help of an editorial assistant, George Simpson, to whom Adorno offers a generous tribute (CM 225–6), he produced four essays: 'A Social Critique of Radio Music'; 'On Popular Music', now one of his most well-known texts; an 'Analytical Study of the NBC *Music Appreciation Hour*'; and 'The Radio Symphony'. However, only the last of these was judged suitable by Lazarsfeld for publication under the auspices of the Princeton project, although 'On Popular Music' was published in the Institute's journal in 1941.

Many of the difficulties which would recur in the subsequent reception of Adorno's work were already evident in his time working on the Princeton project. Indeed, the charges levelled at Adorno's work for the project are those which will follow him throughout his career. Despite his dabbling in empirical research, his approach is heavily methodological in what he distinguishes as the European sense of the word: in America 'methodology' meant discussion of the means for conducting social research. For Adorno, it meant *epistemology*: investigation into the conditions of possibility of knowledge (CM 219). Adorno's more personal writings of this time, such as the materials which later became *Philosophy of Modern Music* (1949), maintain the highly compressed and slightly cryptic style he had first developed in the early 1930s, but are still able to reflect on their own philosophical foundations. Adorno's thought is distinctive in being highly self-reflexive: it always seeks to factor in his own position, rather than pretending to a spuriously neutral stance. With this material stripped away to present apparently more objective and less demanding texts, Adorno's concessions to empirical research have struck critics as unscientific, vague or arbitrary: suspicion abounds that his supposed research really only found what he had already decided he was looking for. Yet when questions of epistemology rather than method do creep in, Adorno undercuts much of what the project for which he is working stands. For example, he comments in his 'Radio Symphony': 'this shows the necessity for starting from the sphere of reproduction of musical works by radio instead of from an analysis of listeners' reactions' (RS 267).

Yet analysis of the audience response was what was expected. No surprise, perhaps, that official response from the sponsors should be extremely dubious: W.G. Preston at NBC commented that Adorno's 'A Social Critique of Radio Music'

> is so full of factual errors and colored opinion, and its pretence at scientific procedure is so absurd in view of its numerous arbitrary assertions, that it is hardly worthy of serious consideration, except possibly as propaganda. In short, it seems to have an axiom to grind.[18]

But then for his own part, Adorno describes the kind of research expected of him as guided by a question 'of *administrative* technique: how to manipulate the masses'.[19] For Adorno, the task of critical thought is to contribute to the emancipation of society as a whole by destroying its pretensions to progress or freedom; but the empirical research he discovered in America was not a protest against the way society is, but an attempt to investigate and understand it, in order to further rationalize it and better control it. Given this tension, little wonder that Adorno and Lazarsfeld were unable to persuade the Rockefeller Foundation to continue to pay for what they wanted, but which Adorno seems unwilling to provide.

Adorno's involvement in empirical social research and his reflections on the theory of sociology continue to manifest these kinds of tensions throughout his career. Although the project on *The Authoritarian Personality*, a study of personality types which sought to estimate the extent to which fascist and anti-Semitic tendencies were present in American society, received considerable acclaim, Adorno's involvement in such work always seems halfhearted, although he knows its importance for the sake of the institute's reputation and finances. When long after the war he was finally made a Professor of Frankfurt University in 1957, Adorno's involvement in research ended almost immediately, although he still lectured on sociology and gave essays and lectures trying to direct the further development of the discipline. Just as he believed philosophy was not separate from the study of history, so the study of society could not proceed without factoring in its own involvement in the rationalization of society it sought to criticize.

The real achievement of Adorno's time in America are the essays he completed with Max Horkheimer, published under the title *Dialectic of Enlightenment: Philosophical Fragments* (1947), and his own books, *Philosophy of Modern Music* and a highly stylized collection of fragments, *Minima Moralia* (1951). In these works Adorno succeeds in synthesizing his critical and aesthetic interests not only with his more abstruse epistemological studies carried out in Oxford, but also with a theoretical account of the interrelationship between philosophy and society. These questions can never again be separated in regard to Adorno's work, and the characteristic density and power of his writing comes from the close interweaving of these three aspects. Adorno followed Horkheimer to Los Angeles in 1941 – although characteristically, he was reluctant to leave his new home in New York – and their close collaboration was productive. He was also writing with a former associate of the Schoenberg circle in Vienna, Hans Eisler, who had moved towards a more directly politicized music under the influence of Brecht (*Composing for the Films* was published, but only under Eisler's name, in 1947); and he was famously consulted by the novelist Thomas Mann, who was working on his own music book, *Dr Faustus*, and in which lengthy extracts from Adorno's manuscripts on music are reproduced verbatim. Compared with the difficult and nomadic years spent travelling between Oxford, Frankfurt and Berlin, and the years of upheaval in Europe during which Adorno lost his close friend Walter Benjamin, who committed suicide in 1940, the time in California seems to have been extraordinarily fruitful. Despite the emphasis subsequent commentators have placed on Adorno's supposed exile, it almost seems as if the further west he travels, the more settled he becomes. Indeed, when the opportunity comes to return to Germany, Adorno strives to keep his options open, spending a year back in Los Angeles in 1952 working on a study of the astrology columns in the *LA Times* in order to maintain the American citizenship which he and his wife only finally relinquish in 1955.

ADORNO'S CULTURAL CRITICISM

This apparent conundrum is worth spending some time unravelling because of the crucial light it can shed on how we understand Adorno's position throughout his mature works. It will mean discussing very quickly some of the arguments which the following chapters will be concerned to substantiate; but it is much easier to start to read and understand Adorno's work if *guided* by the kind of sense of the shape of it as a whole which ought only to be possible *after* such a reading.

To restate the problem: why have so many readers of Adorno understood the time of his physical exile, and in particular his eight years in California (1941–49), as a lowpoint rather than a highpoint in his career? As Peter Hohendahl reports, 'most commentators have rightly stressed its highly problematic nature, either by pointing out how unable and unwilling Adorno was to adjust to the American way of life or by emphasizing how the United States failed to receive and integrate the persona and work of the German-Jewish philosopher'.[20] And admittedly, this is how Adorno appears to present his experience in *Minima Moralia*, his most obviously personal work, written during his time in the USA. The book is subtitled 'Fragments from a damaged life', and it is tempting to misread the book as a documentary account of Adorno's disjunction from his new place of residence. For example, he describes the 'American landscape' as 'uncomforted and comfortless' (MM 28); remarks that 'to the uninformed European, Americans in their entirety can so easily appear as people without dignity' (MM 195); moreover, it is easy to identify what Adorno and Horkheimer called 'the culture industry' in their *Dialectic of Enlightenment* with Hollywood; and the wrong life in which it is impossible to live rightly with the life of America (MM 39).

A tempting reading, but a wrong one. Although Adorno does acknowledge that 'every intellectual in emigration is, without exception, mutilated' (MM 33), *Minima Moralia* is a deeply ironic text, and characteristic of Adorno's presentation of his thought as dialectics at a standstill: formulating incompatible or antagonistic arguments, whose claim on the reader the text refuses to resolve. If Adorno presents himself, in part, as some last remnant of European culture, it is not to damn America by comparison. He certainly means to sharpen the opposition between the European and American way of life, but this is not intended to valorize one over the other. Indeed, looking back over his time in the USA, Adorno comments that he was 'liberated from a naïve belief in culture, acquired the ability to see culture from the outside'. Before his arrival in New York, his belief in the 'absolute and natural importance of spirit was always natural and obvious to me' (CM 239). But the lack of reverence for the works of intellect and spirit he saw in the USA opened his eyes. Rather than confirming a belief in the superiority of the continent he had left behind, Adorno found himself in a new world. The essay in which these claims are made was originally written as a radio broadcast in Germany, so Adorno is not trying to ingratiate himself with his former hosts; if anything, he is praising America in order to indict his homeland. As for Hegel, for whom history moves from east to west, so for most European intellectuals, including Adorno, 'America is therefore the land of the future'.[21] Adorno could feel at home in California because he had stepped into a scenario whose outline already existed for him, and in which the decline of the culture, democratic politics and the triumph of capitalism were inextricably linked.

The schematic connections between these concepts are more fully explored in *Dialectic of Enlightenment*, but we can take a preliminary overview if we bear in mind that both the content and the presentation of Adorno and Horkheimer's book derive in large part from Nietzsche's essays *On the Genealogy of Morality*. For Nietzsche, democracy, based on the principle of equality, is a leveller. It threatens to obliterate the distinctions on which culture depends. Equality itself is a product of what he calls a slave morality, a reactive force based on resentment directed towards aristocratic values, and thus premised on an attack on hierarchy. But the very idea of equality is founded in the experience of commercial exchange. This can be clearly mapped onto Adorno's anxieties in his essays of the 1930s and early 1940s about what he and Horkheimer come to call 'the culture industry' in *Dialectic of Enlightenment*. The capitalist machinery of the distribution and reproduction of culture is a vehicle for the obliteration of both autonomous art and popular art. This meeting in the middle is a kind of entropy, in which the critical value of either form of art is neutralized. The triumph of bourgeois over genuine culture accompanies the domination of capitalism over earlier economic forms, but the idea of the bourgeoisie is more a re-labelling of Nietzsche's 'herd morality' than the product of any strict Marxist analysis. Adorno and Horkheimer differ from Nietzsche in seeing autonomous art as itself a product of bourgeois culture, rather than a remnant of aristocratic values. However, they share with their predecessor an ambiguous relationship to the rise of the bourgeoisie: the very idea of a critical theoretical position depends on the spread of the ideas associated with the Enlightenment; but the triumph of bourgeois rationalism is also the triumph of a mechanical calculation based on the principle of the equivalence of everything, once governed by the principle of exchange.

The significance of America for Adorno is that it is a country in whose modern society there has never been anything *other* than a bourgeoisie. This is the burden of his comments on the Americans appearing to Europeans as a people 'without dignity'. Where class distinction in Germany has been determined 'by whether or not [a man] accepted money', and the receipt of a gift of money prompted shame in the child of a bourgeois family, in America no such reticence exists: 'no child of even well-off parents has inhibitions about earning a few cents by newspaper rounds'. The difference is between a society in which there remain class distinctions, and one in which the supremacy of bourgeois values is total. But Adorno presents this in deeply ambiguous terms – it is a triumph of equality, but it is also the triumph of the principle of the mere equivalence of all things, including people:

> The self-evidence of the maxim that work is no disgrace, the guile-less absence of all snobbery concerning the ignominy, in the feudal sense, of market relationships, the democracy of the earning-principle, contribute to the persistence of what is utterly anti-democratic, economic injustice, human degradation. (MM 195)

Adorno does not resolve this dialectical opposition. It is deliberately unclear whether the reader is intended to agree with one side or the other. The problem this mode of presentation highlights is that the values of culture, which depend on differentiating themselves from the world of commerce, are themselves compromised by their inherent elitism. In setting itself against the sources from which it springs, disavowing its own affinity with the bourgeois and commercial view of the world, culture cuts itself off from the world which it claims to criticize. But without some normative idea of culture as an improved – more moral, more rational – way of life, what values are there against which we might judge the world and find it wanting? Can the choice really be democracy *or* freedom, equality *or* justice?

His liberation from a 'naïve belief in culture' and gaining 'the ability to see culture from the outside' means that Adorno can achieve two otherwise incompatible projects at once. He can criticize American life from the point of view of European culture; but he can also appreciate the challenge to culture represented by the example of American bourgeois democracy. From the perspective of the Weimar prophets of crisis, without culture there must be either unending disaster or apocalyptic reinvention. But in America, Adorno discovers instead . . . democracy. What is expressed as a contrast in *Minima Moralia* is more fully spelt out in the later essay: what was imposed on Germany rather late as 'nothing more than the formal rules of the game' is there deep-rooted, 'substantial'.

The political form of democracy is infinitely closer to the people. American everyday life, despite the oft lamented hustle and bustle, has an inherent element of peaceableness, good-naturedness, and generosity, in sharpest contrast to the pent-up malice and envy which exploded in Germany between 1933 and 1945. (CM 240)

Adorno is no starry-eyed optimist, having studied not only authoritarian tendencies amongst the American population, but carried out research into new breeds of irrationalism being exploited by the right-wing and anti-Semitic radio preacher Martin Thomas, or exemplified in the astrology columns of the *LA Times*.[22] He knows that 'America is no longer the land of unlimited possibilities' (CM 240). Indeed we might even take the opposition between American and European values as being more figurative than actual. We noted earlier a comment from 1929 which already suggests that the key to critical thinking is to look from within and without at the same time, with both the knowledge and authority of the musical expert and the innocent wonder of the child: is Adorno here giving the names of 'Europe' and 'America' to the same positions, inside and outside culture? Yet this still gives a good provisional understanding of the difficulties of Adorno's position. The culture on which it had prided itself did not prevent Germany from collapsing into barbarism; nor did the artistic avant-gardes. Seen only from within, this could only lead to a sense of crisis and catastrophe. But coming to terms with America means facing the possibility that 'the concept of culture in which one has grown up has . . . itself become obsolete' (CM 241). It means looking at culture from the inside, as a project doomed to perpetuate itself only through vicious and violent contradictions; but also from the outside, as a determined historical and political project, and therefore neither a natural nor the only possible one.

Adorno's attempt to find a way of thinking and a form of expression adequate to this situation takes him to a complex combination of Hegel and Nietzsche, the two thinkers he acknowledges as the most penetrating thinkers of the dialectic of enlightenment: the idea that rationality, in seeking to overcome irrational understandings of the world, itself turns into a form of irrational domination. From Hegel, he receives his sense that to think dialectically is to present the negation of negation. What appears as a false world when judged from the point of view of culture is to be shattered through confrontation with its own contradictions; while at the same time the possibility of such a critique is itself put into question through being brought into contact with a sense of its own necessary limits. Through this process of self-critical reasoning, culture seeks to reinvent itself from within, while the possibility that the new will come from outside it is left open. In this Adorno shares some of Nietzsche's longing for a revaluation of all values. But where Nietzsche tends to fear the levelling force of bourgeois equality, Adorno refuses to rush to judgement. He cannot embrace the destruction of culture, since that would mean affirming its untruth, from culture's point of view. But his mourning of culture is always tinged with the knowledge that something else may be beyond its demise. This is a problem which cannot be resolved by the individual thinker. The answer can only emerge in the course of history. Like Hegel, Adorno does not believe that the task of the philosopher is to predict the future, but to interpret the present in relation to the past. Or in terms taken from Lukács, to shatter the world of 'second nature' by proving it to be the product of historical forces, but without claiming to have recovered an original world of first nature behind it. In passing to a land founded upon the bourgeois culture whose victory is nearly complete in Europe, Adorno is passing into the realm of what might seem to be his worst fears, but which may always turn out to be his best hopes.

This position leads to the strange and uncanny ambivalence of Adorno's cultural criticism which contributes so much to its difficulty for the reader. It is often hard to locate Adorno's argument because he does not take a single position but juxtaposes two or more. The essay titled simply 'Cultural Criticism and Society', which stands at the beginning of his collection *Prisms*, suggesting that it might serve as a manifesto for the essays on particular topics within the book, is typically ambiguous. Adorno does not declare himself for or against cultural criticism; in fact one might say that no single statement or argument in the essay is itself a summation of his position. Rather Adorno attempts to model the dialectical tensions between – in this case – immanent and transcendental versions of critique. Should society be criticized from the standpoint of culture, or culture seen as serving a particular function in society, therefore invalidating its claim to have transcended the social world? Neither answer is wholly adequate, because incomplete. But nor does Adorno resolve the dialectic into some fuller model of intellectual endeavour: the two arguments are simply juxtaposed, as if to bring out and intensify their antagonism.

In his essay on Oswald Spengler in the same collection, a similar ambiguity is evident. Adorno neither confirms nor denies Spengler's pessimistic account in *The Decline of the West* (1926) of the collapse of 'culture' into what the German language stigmatizes as mere 'civilization'. It is almost difficult to overestimate the success of Spengler's work, which sold millions of copies, and which was also widely read in Britain and the United States. The analyses of decline, degeneration and decay which gave a morbid thrill to the intellectual classes of the early twentieth century draw largely on the inheritance of the Romantic revolt against reason: they are symptoms of the intense ambivalence which attaches to the idea of culture, once society is seen as standing in opposition to some more natural way of existing. Adorno's response throughout his life is not to try and refute these arguments by proving that modern life is somehow better than has been claimed; nor will he repeat the Romantic reaction which seeks to valorize archaic forms of society in opposition to the soul-less modern world. The idea of organic form, the desire for natural community, the perceived loss of spontaneous feeling: these are symptoms of the decline, rather than its remedy. Adorno's strategy is to sustain such criticism of the modern world, but to juxtapose it with criticism of any proposed solutions. By matching a negative with another negative, as it were, rather than seeking to replace it with a false positive, Adorno hopes to release an image of what else might be possible. As he puts it in the Spengler essay, 'what can oppose the decline of the west is not a resurrected culture but the utopia that is silently contained in the image of its decline' (P 72).

Adorno's work needs to be understood not as the last gasp of a dying culture, but as the vital self-critical dismantling of that culture from within, confronted by its own irreconcilable contradictions. As we will see in the following chapters, this can be traced through Adorno's work on aesthetics, moral philosophy and metaphysics: in each case, a philosophical account of art, of morality and of truth is brought to its limit. Adorno does not reject philosophy: only a rational approach can answer certain kinds of questions about the validity of the categories with which we interpret the world, but

there is room in his work for a certain amount of scepticism concerning the demand that philosophy transform the world. As a
working hypothesis, the idea of the rational emancipation of each
individual, the classic ideal of culture and of enlightenment, is less
objectionable than any other proposed solution to the perceived
crisis of modernity, particularly those which seek to fuse the individual into a single irrational social or political body. But there is a
sense in Adorno's work that actually this solution, the best yet proposed, might always turn out to be the real problem, and hence there
is a hint of an anarchistic rejection of the value of culture itself. If
he were to openly voice such a demand, Adorno would seem to be
legitimating the irrational destruction of culture which would not
replace it with anything better, but only the tyranny of barbarism.
As a result, he can only endorse the continual self-criticism of
culture. So Adorno does not quite give up on the idea of culture,
which is also that of reason, autonomy and justice; but certainly the
possible destruction of culture can never again seem like the end of
everything.

Adorno's idea of cultural criticism is certainly stamped by his experience in the United States, but what he learns is not to reject that
which is outside his idea of culture; rather the opposite, he seeks to
make space in his thought for that which might come from outside.
American democracy may be the mere equivalence of everyone
without hierarchy. Unlike many of Nietzsche's heirs, including
Heidegger and those American Nietzscheans who follow Leo Strauss,
who see this as the triumph of herd morality over aristocratic virtues
which make true dwelling on the earth impossible, Adorno hopes for
a rather different sort of future, neither home-coming or disaster, but
something more like a release from the dialectics of culture altogether.

RETURN

If America had given Adorno a lesson in democracy, it had prepared
him for the most important upheaval of his life. For the most
significant of Adorno's successive emigrations is his final one, the shift
of the American citizen to an alien and forbidding country which
cannot properly be called a return, since Germany is no longer his
home. An over-emphasis on Adorno's exile ignores the most difficult
political decision of his life. What distinguishes Adorno and
Horkheimer from almost all their other friends and colleagues who

had been forced to flee to the United States is the simple fact of their return to Europe. Herbert Marcuse, Siegfried Kracauer, and many other figures closely or loosely associated with the Institute for Social Research, never made it back. Nor did other well-known intellectuals such as Hannah Arendt. Having made new homes in the USA, many were to play an influential role in the development of post-war culture in America. By contrast, Adorno and Horkheimer chose a different path, and opted to play a part in the reconstruction of Germany after the material and psychic devastation wrought by the Nazi regime, by the Second World War and by the Holocaust.

This was anything but a soft option. The decision by Horkheimer and Adorno to seek to re-establish the Institute for Social Research in Frankfurt in 1950 was a calculated political strategy as to how they might best engage in the reconstruction of post-war West Germany and work to avoid a repetition of the evils of the Nazi regime. The twenty-year period from 1950 to the late 1960s has been judged harshly by the self-proclaimed inheritors of Adorno and Horkheimer. It is axiomatic that history has invariably been written from the standpoint of the victors. In the immediate aftermath of Adorno's death, this was certainly the case. Rolf Wiggerhaus's history of the Frankfurt School sees this period as one of decline and hibernation. Certainly, the critical decision to work towards the construction of a democracy in West Germany which would actually survive the strains and stresses of the post-war era, unlike its ill-fated Weimar predecessor, looks like a political cop-out from the perspective of 60s radicalism. In the years preceding his death, Adorno was engaged in a running conflict with student activists, perplexed by his apparent refusal to support the kind of revolutionary activities they felt his work demanded. On 31 January 1969, 76 students were arrested when Adorno called the police to the offices of the Institute for Social Research. Until he suspended his classes later that year Adorno was a high-profile target, perhaps because, as he suggested in an interview, his lectures attracted so many students.[23]

What is striking is the degree to which the radical students of the era share this evaluation with Adorno and Horkheimer's intellectual heirs. Both perceive a mismatch between the critical theory being developed during the 1930s in the discussions of the Institute, and in its journal, and the two men now in charge. Extracts from older writings by both were copied and pasted up on posters, or distributed in leaflets: an exercise in immanent critique, perhaps, in which onlookers were invited to measure the truth of the two men's actions against their earlier ideas. Both the students and the younger generation of the Frankfurt School scholars wished to turn back the clock, and to reverse Adorno and Horkheimer's intellectual development. Their radical opponents wanted to recover the revolutionary fervour of the late Weimar and early Nazi era; their colleagues the idea of a total social theory. What this really meant was the attempt to get around Adorno's more sceptical influence, to reach the Horkheimer who had written such programmatic essays as 'Traditional and Critical Theory', in which a revolutionary politics and a radical theory of society went hand in hand. This must mean regressing behind the rigour of the subsequent insight, central to *Dialectic of Enlightenment*, that the idea of a theory of society contributes to social rationalization, rather than breaking its spell. That this realization is what *enabled* the political interventions of Horkheimer and Adorno seems to have escaped everyone's notice.

It is in fact arguable whether there was ever a central core of ideas which could be labelled 'critical theory'. Agnes Heller has argued that 'the resurrection of the Frankfurt School as a school came in the sixties, with the reemergence of a cause, or rather of several causes. It was in the sixties that the name "the Frankfurt School" was invented, first in America'.[24] The implication is that this was largely political myth-making. The reanimation of the Frankfurt School was more like the conjuring of a ghost; not just a reminder of a past that Horkheimer in particular, whose radical rhetoric had been more shrill, wished to put behind him, but the invention of a comprehensive theoretical position which had never existed. Leo Lowenthal comments acerbically in an interview that Horkheimer had never conceived of an all-embracing social theory, no matter what the publication of a book titled 'Critical Theory' might suggest. In her own essay published in 2002, Heller suggests that those times 'are gone again'.[25] A self-proclaimed Critical Theorist in the 1970s and 1980s needed to shrug off Adorno's ghost, while seeking at the same time to establish oneself as a legitimate successor by taking on the mantle of his theoretical authority. That at least seems the project of Habermas's *Philosophical Discourse of Modernity*, in which Habermas argues that Adorno and Horkheimer leave themselves no way out except backwards: the step he must take in order to begin a reconstruction.

However, it is now becoming less clear that the dismissive claim made by Habermas that 'the old Frankfurt School never took bourgeois democracy very seriously' can be seriously sustained.[26] In fact it takes very little effort to reconstruct Adorno's arguments. True democracy can only come through the autonomy of the individual members of a society, an autonomy which cannot be imposed from above, but can only be developed through education. This demands both a commitment to reform of those institutions which fail to promote such autonomy, and the encouragement of the kind of critical self-reflective thought which Adorno recommends. Alongside the critique of the culture industry which 'impedes the development of autonomous, independent individuals who judge and decide consciously for themselves' these 'would be the precondition of a democratic society which needs adults who have come of age in order to sustain itself and develop' (CI 106). Politically this means a commitment to 'democracy through representation, to which even the experts in the administration of cultural matters owe their legitimation' on the grounds that it 'permits a certain balance; it makes possible the hindrance of manoeuvres which serve barbarism through the corruption of the idea of objective quality by means of callous appeal to the common will' (CI 129). The lessons of the 1930s are evidently fixed in Adorno's mind. Attacking the conditions which restrict people's ability to think independently, attacking the substitution of the will of the people for the decisions of individuals, attacking the idea that politics might be simply abolished by revolution in favour of a new vision of mankind, as if any such vision would not be deeply marked by that to which it was opposed: these are the critical interventions which might help prolong and stabilize Germany's democratic situation. As for the students who demanded some kind of authority to back their sloganeering, Adorno reminds an interviewer that 'in my writings, I have never offered a model for any kind of action for some specific campaign . . . my thinking has always stood in a rather indirect relationship to praxis'. In a pair of late essays, 'Marginalia on Theory and Praxis' and 'Resignation' (both 1969), Adorno revisits what has always been a central part of his theory: that the drive to action, the insistence on activism, is itself a threat to theoretical reflection – which alone allows the possibility of rational autonomy – and slides far faster to irrationalism than theory can. It is hard to see how Habermas can reasonably construe this, as he does in

The Philosophical Discourse of Modernity, as giving up on the rationalist inheritance of the Enlightenment.

As Max Pensky argues, the thesis that Adorno and Horkheimer conceived of their work as a 'message in a bottle', addressed to an uncertain future which alone might bring redemption, with no hope of change in the present, is beginning to be revised. Reviewing a monumental study by Alex Demirovic, Pensky suggests that not only were Adorno and Horkheimer public intellectuals, contributing essays and lectures and public appearances wherever possible, but that behind the scenes there was an incredible amount of tedious committee work to drawing up reports and programmes, to enact a series of pedagogical reforms, to steer the development of sociology as a discipline in Germany, and to break down the idea of the academic as a neutral observer, producing new models of engagement:

> Rather than hermetically protecting an emphatic notion of truth from a society that is untrue as a whole, Horkheimer and Adorno were in fact conducting what Foucault referred to as a politics of truth: operating in, below and between public spheres, they effectively challenged the terms and procedures through which socially valid truths were constructed, where the rules of truth-production were legitimated, where rhetorics or vocabularies were approved and subjects authorized.[27]

While one may with hindsight wish to argue that particular decisions made by Adorno and Horkheimer were wrong, it is difficult to claim that there was a turn away from politics in their work: if anything, there is a turn towards it.

But this is also to ignore the tremendous outpouring of prose from Adorno. Throughout the last twenty years of his life, he was incredibly productive, writing on literature (three volumes of *Notes on Literature* in his lifetime (1958, 1961, 1965), one posthumous (1974)), sociology, philosophy and, as ever, music. Moreover, Adorno took great steps to ensure that his work was being disseminated as widely as possible. While much of his written work is as stylized and complex as the earlier texts, he also gave dozens of lectures and talks on radio, many of which were republished in collections of essays under the broad heading of 'Critical Models'. As Henry Pickford argues in the introduction to the English translation of many of these talks, Adorno was not only concerned to communicate as clearly as possible

with the wide audience made available through modern telecommuni-
cations, but to publish his works in popular journals and in paperback:
'his engagement in the mass media was a logical consequence of his
eminently practical intentions to effect change'.[28] Adorno saw himself
as a public intellectual: he both accepts and acknowledges his own
entanglement in the same 'culture industry' that he not only anato-
mizes but criticizes relentlessly, repetitively, almost tediously; an
entanglement that is the necessary price of any attempt to intervene.
Permanent exile would be easy by comparison. Certain themes return
again and again in Adorno's public interventions: the need to ensure
events never repeat themselves; the need to develop a deep-rooted
democratic culture; the need to avoid positivist or technicist thinking;
the importance of culture but the impoverishment of what passes for
it; administration and systematization which passes from top to
bottom of society, in which the thinker is entwined.

Most of all, however, there are two remarkable books on which
much of Adorno's philosophical and critical legacy depends. *Negative
Dialectics* (1966) – which consolidates and expands on his earlier
Against Epistemology: A Metacritique (1956), built around his Oxford
Husserl studies – is Adorno's most extended attempt to provide a
basis for a non-systematic philosophy. Unlike the ironically presented
Minima Moralia and the genealogical *Dialectic of Enlightenment*, it is
a more straightforward work of philosophy, albeit fairly idiosyncratic, consisting on the one hand of detailed criticisms of Heidegger,
Kant and Hegel, and on the other reflections on the very possibility
of philosophy after Auschwitz. Its counterpart is *Aesthetic Theory*
(1970), still unrevised when Adorno died, but published shortly after-
wards. These works deliberately refuse a systematic form: as Adorno
told his students in one of his lectures, he belonged 'to a generation
that grew up in violent rebellion against the very concept of metaphysical systems, and whose entire way of thinking was defined by
that rebellion' (PMP 20). Indeed, because of its relentlessly critical
nature, it might be easier to think of Adorno's thought as more like a
pattern of interference within more traditional philosophy than as a
distinct philosophical approach of its own.

AFTERMATH

By the time of his death it was clear that Adorno's ideas, always
untimely, had not found a comfortable place in the world. In the

years preceding his death in 1969, Adorno was denounced by student activists for failing to support their demands and by the media for failing to condemn them. In the heated political atmosphere at the University of Frankfurt in the 60s, the scholars of the Institute for Social Research were attacked from both sides. These complaints linger on to this day as common currency in what ought to have been Adorno's natural constituencies, the academy, leftist politics and the European cultural and political elites: that his work is esoteric, hermetic, a withdrawal from rather than an engagement with the world. His students wanted revolutionary slogans, but Adorno offered them only a course entitled 'An Introduction to Dialectical Thinking', suspended in April 1969 after Adorno was assaulted at his podium by topless female students. Whereas his former colleague Herbert Marcuse became one of the leading lights of the New Left, Adorno was more than happy – proud even – to admit in a newspaper interview that he was working on a book of aesthetics.[29] Adorno's friend and inspiration Walter Benjamin once called for a 'politicization' of aesthetics in response to fascism's aestheticization of politics; unkind commentators have seen Adorno's course as neither, merely a retreat from politics to art. While Benjamin's work has been widely fêted over the course of the last twenty years, Adorno remains misunderstood and maligned, in his own Germany as much as abroad. It is often claimed that to read German is a necessary condition for understanding Adorno. Even if that were true, the response in his homeland suggests that it can by no means be a sufficient one.

Subsequent developments in European and American thought and society continue to show Adorno's work in an awkward light. Adorno's scepticism towards the idea of progress, his interest in the non-identical, i.e. his interest in the extent to which reality resists being understood or appropriated by conceptual thought, and his critique of the priority of the subject, prefigure similar concerns in the work of a younger generation of French thinkers, such as Derrida and Foucault, whose major works were beginning to be published in the last years of Adorno's life. But since these concerns are rooted in a common inheritance from earlier philosophies, as recent studies of German Idealism and early Romantic philosophy have shown, these connections are not a question of direct inspiration. Furthermore, the inspiration of Heidegger on such thinkers would have appalled Adorno, who consistently criticized the latter's philosophy and politics. Adorno's Marxism is equally provoking: his anti-communism distancing him from other intellectuals such as Ernst Bloch or Bertolt Brecht who had chosen to commit themselves to the building of a socialist state in East Germany; his commitment to Marxism making him suspect from the perspective of the USA. Adorno contributed to CIA-sponsored journals in the years of reconstruction in Germany; but the FBI kept files on him when he was in the USA. The generation of German philosophers and social theorists which succeeded Adorno's have generally disowned his work. His insistence on the threat of fascism within apparently democratic societies, his unwavering stress on the devastating philosophical impact of the Holocaust, and his scepticism about the likely improvement of society through technical or scientific development look even more like an attempt to swim against the current today, 36 years after his death.

Pip, the protagonist of Charles Dickens's *Great Expectations*, tells the reader in the novel's opening pages that he used to try and imagine what his parents must have been like based only on the evidence of the lettering of their names on their gravestones. It sometimes seems as if many of Adorno's critics have formed their impression of his work on a similar principle, judging him by the appearance of his prose on the page: dense, morbid, gloomy and patrician. Adorno's style can be formidable: the characteristic unit of his thought and of his writing is the paragraph, as he turns ideas over and over, rotating them into conjunction with different concepts. Long sentences mean long paragraphs, sometimes unbroken by subheadings. His writing can be dense and tangled, arguments as starkly stated as his sentences are wreathed in qualifying clauses, making little concession to direct exposition, or to signposts for the reader. While English-language publishers, reluctant to adhere to Adorno's principles of composition, often break up paragraphs or introduce subheadings, the ink on the pages of the German editions lies thick and dense.

If Adorno's exile has been prolonged, it may well be because, as Said notes in another essay, his style is 'dense and extremely involuted'. 'It is', he accepts, 'very easy to be impatient with this sort of writing.'[30] Certainly, Adorno has had a great many impatient readers. Unlike the works of his philosophical nemesis Martin Heidegger, Adorno's collected works are available in German in a cheap paperback edition – a small victory, perhaps. At the time of writing, all

20 volumes (23 books in total) can be yours for only €200. (Subsequent publication of posthumous works, including unfinished work reconstructed from Adorno's notes and transcripts of his lecture courses, may add more than twenty volumes to his oeuvre.) Blue pocket-sized tombstones, packed with dense text on thin paper, published in Frankfurt, they testify to both Adorno's productive relationship with the publisher Peter Suhrkamp, and his lifelong association with the regional city. They testify to his hopes that critical thought need not be a privilege confined to an intellectual elite, and remind us of his pleasure at the rapid sales of a Suhrkamp series: Bloch, Benjamin and Adorno in paperback; and being sold on station bookstalls![31] Yet the commercial availability of Adorno's work contrasts starkly with its accessibility. Writing on moral philosophy, epistemology, sociology, aesthetics, literature and, above all, music, Adorno's works are not only formidable in length, breadth and erudition but deeply idiosyncratic in approach. The aim of this *Guide for the Perplexed* is to help make Adorno's work more readable. In this chapter I hope to have set out something of the broad framework within which his writings on art and culture, on freedom and society, and on philosophy and history can be read, while the following chapters turn to each of these areas in more detail.

CHAPTER 2

ART AND CULTURE

The dialectical critic of culture must both participate in culture and not participate. Only then does he do justice to his object and to himself.

(P 33)

Important works of art are the ones that aim for an extreme; they are destroyed in the process and their broken outlines survive as the ciphers of a supreme, unnameable truth.

(QF 226)

The close identification of a critic with a particular artist or movement can often be telling. In Adorno's case, a long association with the composer Arnold Schoenberg reveals a great deal about his approach not only to art and culture, but also to philosophy and criticism in general. Adorno first met Schoenberg through the latter's pupil Alban Berg, with whom he took composition lessons in 1925, and subsequently maintained contact until Berg's death ten years later. A letter to Kracauer suggests Adorno's ambivalence towards his musical master at this time: 'there's something uncanny and oppressive about the chap', he writes; and he goes on to record his shock at the similarity between Schoenberg's handwriting and his own.[1] Adorno undoubtedly flatters himself through the comparison. Relations between the two were never more than cordial, and Schoenberg could often be irritated by the attentions of this earnest young German whose appreciation of his work came wrapped in such an esoteric and speculative philosophical apparatus. After the publication of *Philosophy of Modern Music* in 1949, and already annoyed by the appearance of his ideas in Thomas Mann's *Dr Faustus* thanks to Adorno's collaboration with the novelist, Schoenberg commented that Adorno had 'clearly never liked my music'.[2] Nothing could be further from the truth: Adorno's enthusiasm for the work of the older man lays the foundation for his conception of what contemporary art could be; and even of what it should be. A greater tribute perhaps is the fact that to understand what Adorno hears in Schoenberg can help us appreciate why his own writings deliberately take such a dense and unfamiliar form.

Schoenberg is best known for his break with conventional tonality in music, and his subsequent development of the 'twelve-tone' system. Where most western classical music of the eighteenth and nineteenth centuries had been organized around a conventional set of relationships between notes at particular points on the musical scale, atonal music sought a greater fluidity and freedom through refusing to settle into such pre-determined patterns. Rather than imposing a rigid 'system' on his composition, working with twelve tones in fact allowed Schoenberg to create work which moved more freely and more dramatically away from conventional musical forms. In a retrospective essay, this is the aspect of the composer's work which Adorno stresses. Because of its importance to Adorno's interpretation of Schoenberg, and so to our understanding of Adorno, it is worth quoting at length:

> The difference between Schoenberg and traditional music might be demonstrated with the help of a *bon mot* of Schumann's that one can tell whether a person is musical by his ability to continue performing a piece more or less correctly when someone forgets to turn the page. This, precisely, is not possible in the case of Schoenberg. By no means because his music is 'not music', is chaotic and governed by chance. Rather traditional music was stamped through and through by the schema of tonality; it moved within harmonic, melodic, and formal paths that were pre-drawn by this schema. It was as if every musical particular was subordinated to an established generality. By listening appropriately, starting from there, one would be able to deduce the development of its particulars in detail and find one's way with relative ease. Traditional music listened for the listener. This, precisely, is over and done with in Schoenberg. The musical context wants to be understood purely from within itself, without lightening the listener's burden by means of an already available system of coordinates within which the particular is nothing but minimal variation. (EOM 629–30)

Adorno stresses that Schoenberg's innovation is not a rejection of tradition so much as an extension of it, an exploration of a possibility that was already inherent within western music, but restrained until then by various formal conventions. Schoenberg does not impose a new set of abstract formulae on his music as later serial composers were tempted to do – 'musicians are usually truants from maths classes,' quips Adorno, 'it would be a terrible fate for them to end up in the hands of the maths teacher after all' (QF 269) – but liberates the individual moments of his composition from their subordination to the whole: 'In this music, the only thing that still matters is the particular, the now and here of the musical events, their own inner logic' (EOM 630).

A comparison with Adorno's own work is helpful. Like Schoenberg, Adorno's work on aesthetics will make little sense unless understood in the light of the specific tradition from which it distinguishes itself by its own innovations. Adorno's *Aesthetic Theory* does not start from scratch and attempt to build an aesthetic theory from the ground up, but explores ambiguities, tensions and possibilities present in received ideas of art and culture, just as Schoenberg's later twelve-tone system is not a methodology so much as an attempt to consolidate a way of composing which has been led by the musical material itself. Heard in the light of subsequent and more radical experiments in the use of noise, repetition and chance in composition, it can be difficult, looking back, to see what all the fuss was about Schoenberg's work. Equally, Adorno's work can look as if it remains too indebted to the tradition which it seeks to put into question to constitute a sufficient break with it. As we will see, this is because Adorno senses that the simple rejection of the claims made on behalf of art, as with other supposedly radical revisions of the concept of culture, are neither particularly interesting nor politically and socially progressive. Finally, it is worth noting that Adorno's own work will itself seek to be aesthetic in a certain way. This does not mean that Adorno aims to create art rather than philosophy, but that the attention to the particular, to the here and now of specific events, which he discerns in Schoenberg's work, is also his own objective. Adorno seeks a way of thinking and writing which continually explores the tension between the necessary generalization involved in conceptual thought and the singularity and particularity of thought's objects: that is, of the world.

So if Adorno's writing might be described as aesthetic, we need to be careful that this does not become dismissive – as if to say he is concerned with art rather than something else: politics say, or society. For Adorno all these questions are intertwined; but this is not because he seeks to politicize art, but rather to explore the inevitable entanglement of art and politics which has always already begun. But it is more important to see that Adorno's thought is aesthetic in the sense that it is concerned with the singular: torn between a wish to allow the object to stand alone without the intervention of thought, concepts, reason, and the knowledge that such unmediated access to the object is impossible. In *Negative Dialectics* Adorno suggests that critical philosophy and autonomous art share a common aspiration towards singularity – the 'now and here' of all events, not just musical ones. But art strives to achieve this by its radical resistance to determination, meaning, explanation; philosophy can only pass by way of the concept, and thus through mediation (ND 15). This means an inevitable conflict, attested to in the common feeling that theoretical or philosophical investigation is somehow inimical to art, between the art work's claim to sensuous immediacy, to freedom from conceptual determination, and philosophy's rejection of that claim. Adorno has to find a way to relate these positions, and to allow the art work's inexhaustibility, its final impenetrability to analysis, to emerge within the work of the critic and theorist, without reverting to a simple affirmation of irrationality. In the critique of any claim to immediate aesthetic experience and the argument that any perception of an art work is always mediated by the concept of art Adorno carries through his political suspicion of the appeal to authenticity in his own criticism.

To be successful in Adorno's terms, there must be a perpetual tension within Schoenberg's works between the unity of an individual piece and the musical materials from which it is made. Similarly, Adorno sees thought itself as a struggle by the mind to reduce the world to knowable, repeatable elements, in order to explain and understand it. His task is to find a form for thinking in which this struggle is not resolved one-sidedly in the subordination of the objects of thought by the pattern imposed upon them by the thinker. Aesthetics has proved a challenge to philosophy precisely because it concerns the synthesis of unique and in principle unrepeatable sensations of pleasure or of taste with the universality and necessity of the truth philosophy claims to uncover. A theory of aesthetics is always going to be paradoxical or contradictory, in claiming to account for what must, by definition, remain exceptional. What characterizes

Adorno's writing is the effort to explore rather than reason away such obstacles.

This accounts for some of the difficulty of reconstructing Adorno's thoughts on art and culture. Other difficulties come from the unsystematic presentation of his work in this area. Adorno wrote countless short essays and reviews for magazines and newspapers, testimonies to the occasional nature of criticism; other pieces, although collected in volumes of literary and musical writings, are equally addressed to a particular publication or event. Abstracted from their specific temporal and spatial occasion, a reader needs to expend considerable effort in reconstructing their context in order to get some sense of the specific force of each intervention. Part of the dialectical quality of Adorno's work is that it is very often a response – to what passes for common sense at the time of writing, to a specific claim made about a work, or to quite specific developments in particular artistic traditions – and so it helps to know something of the situation to appreciate Adorno's point. This tension is reversed in the thorny maze of *Aesthetic Theory*, which although incomplete at the time of his death, is the most intense expression of Adorno's own quest for form. The ambiguous title offers us both sides of Adorno's project: a theory of the aesthetic which must struggle to come to terms with the violence of arraigning the singularity of the art work under general categories, and a theory which itself aspires to the uniqueness and individuality of the art work. Part of the strangeness of *Aesthetic Theory* is that a work on the concept of art should make so little direct reference to specific works. But this lacuna is understandable, because the last kind of legacy Adorno would have wished to bequeath us would be a list of 'approved' works, rather than a sense of the criteria on which the specific historical moment of a work might be judged. At the heart of his theory of aesthetics lies the puzzling notion of 'truth-content', which for Adorno is always a question of the *historicity* of the work of art: something like the 'now and here' of the musical events in Schoenberg's pieces.

Just as nothing is immediately given for Adorno, so there are no definitive beginnings in his work. Rather than try to give Adorno's account of aesthetics a more systematic form than it aspires to, I have chosen to explore it through a question which was never of central concern to Adorno himself, but has become a key controversy in subsequent discussions of how to respond to his work. Accordingly, this chapter has been designed to explore the connections and tensions between Adorno's treatment of autonomous art and his assessment of popular culture. In the first section I show that Adorno's criticisms of popular music are primarily formal: they are based on the structure and types of work, and not principally on social grounds. The formal distinction between standardized and non-standardized art is shown in the second section to derive from Adorno's dependence on the Romantic tradition of aesthetics, which dictates his approval of autonomous art and his opposition to 'committed' art. The consequences of this for Adorno's evaluation of art are drawn out in the third section by relating Adorno's argument to the art of his times, and with reference to the distinction now often drawn by critics between modernist and avant-garde art. The key point throughout the chapter is that the specific link between aesthetics and freedom in which Adorno is interested depends on the historical possibility of autonomous art: but in the fourth section I argue that Adorno's understanding of the task of criticism does not preclude an analysis of what he calls 'truth-content' in popular culture as well as autonomous art. This in turn clarifies the idea of 'the culture industry', a term which condenses Adorno's historical and philosophical analysis of the contemporary situation for both popular and autonomous art, to be examined in the fifth section. Finally I conclude by arguing for the continued relevance of this account of art and culture, distinguishing Adorno's historical approach from that of more recent historicist criticism.

ADORNO AND POPULAR MUSIC

Adorno often remarks on the shock of Schoenberg's work for its first audiences, and the same problem seems to accompany his own writing. An early reviewer of his 'Radio Symphony' essay commented: 'I find it difficult to write temperately about the motivation, the method, the results of the Adorno performance – of the aggressive ostentation and triumphant assurance in the display of his powers that leap out at one from his use of one of the methods of the German system-grinders and concept-spinners to produce the conclusions.' Clearly Adorno had got under his skin, for the same writer complained again later that same year (1942) about 'the combination of its pedantic fact-grubbing with a concept-spinning so freed from connection with fact, sometimes, as to become utterly fantastic, and indeed often manipulating facts, and misrepresenting them for its purposes'.[3] What is remarkable is not the vehemence of this response, but how typical it remains of many readers' reactions. Adorno is best known in the English-speaking world for his writing on popular culture, mostly produced in the years of exile in the United States, despite the fact that it is a very small part of his philosophical and critical achievement. Or perhaps it would be more accurate to say 'notorious', since for the most part Adorno's name is simply used as shorthand for an elitist contempt for mass culture with which 'we' are assumed to have little in common. Part of my aim in this chapter is to demonstrate that this conclusion is unjust. Indeed, Adorno deserves more credit for the fact that he always saw the whole of society as worthy of the careful historical and aesthetic scrutiny he saw as the task of philosophy, without deciding as to the significance of any of its aspects in advance: it is a short step from his proclamation that 'the matters of true philosophical interest at this point in history' are 'nonconceptuality, individuality and particularity – things which ever since Plato used to be dismissed as transitory and insignificant' (ND 8) to taking seriously the most ephemeral and supposedly worthless elements of social life.

Only two of the four essays written in the United States while Adorno was working on the Princeton Radio Project, and which crystallize his views on popular culture, were published at that time: 'The Radio Symphony', which provoked the perplexed outburst cited above; and 'On Popular Music', which has since become widely anthologized as an example of Adorno's views. Taken together they do provide a reasonable introduction to Adorno's approach, but we should note that while in a number of ways they are quite typical of his work in this area, in other ways they are rather different. The fact that they were originally written in English rather than German means that Adorno has to rein in those aspects of his style which consist in exploiting the resonances of particular phrases or words of his native tongue. Moreover, because they were originally part of the projected outcomes of the research project they have a curiously neutral tone, as if prepared primarily for the project's corporate sponsors, which sits uneasily with Adorno's usual way of working. Adorno much prefers to push his arguments to extremes, partly in response to his understanding of the way thought must overcome its own sedentary tendencies, but also partly in order to force some kind of response from the reader. So neither essay displays the acerbic bite of Adorno's notorious essay 'On Jazz', written while he was in England,

and published under the name of Hektor Rottweiler, in which he sets out to demolish a whole range of myths surrounding the commercial European jazz music of the 1920s and 1930s. Adorno argues that jazz is neither as new nor as complex as it claims; that its supposed libidinous vitality depends on a myth of racial primitivism and masks its function as a marker of social authority; that its popularity with the proletariat is led by aspirational imitation of an art form primarily produced for the bourgeoisie.

Where in 'On Jazz' Adorno had snarled and menaced, trying to reveal the gap between what people told themselves about jazz and its actual functional and commodity character, the most striking feature of 'On Popular Music' is its even-handedness. Adorno takes the division between 'popular' and 'serious' music as his starting point not in order to reinforce it, but to examine its social function and assess whether it has a musical basis. So Adorno does not divide music up according to its listeners; and he explicitly states that the difference should not be expressed in terms which tend to imply some kind of value: ' "highbrow and lowbrow," "simple and complex," "naïve and sophisticated" ' (OPM 441). Although he doesn't expand on this, such terms would imply that the relationship between popular and serious music is a natural and inevitable one, and that there was some simple progression from the lower to the higher art form. By contrast, the distinction which Adorno prefers is that between standardized and non-standardized music, and refers to the way the music is designed to affect the listener (OPM 437–8, 442–4). In standardized music, the whole of the piece is dominant over its parts, or put simply, because the piece conforms to their expectations, the listener always knows what's coming next; in non-standardized music, exemplified for Adorno by the work of Schoenberg, this is not the case. There is a tension between each part and the whole, rather than the part fitting in like 'a cog in a machine' (OPM 440). As Adorno suggests in his earlier essay 'On the Social Situation of Music', the success of Schoenberg might be judged by the shock which greets his work (EOM 396), the shock of the new which characterizes all autonomous art.

That Adorno considers this formal aspect of non-standardized music to be what makes it different from popular music, but also what gives it a certain kind of value, is clear from his analysis of the effect of broadcasting on complex orchestral music in 'The Radio Symphony'. A Beethoven symphony, Adorno argues, is characterized by the relationships between the various elements of the work, and between those elements and its unity as a whole. It is these relationships in which he is particularly interested, and the extent to which they are threatened by the radio transmission of the symphony, as well as the degree to which the tensions of the symphony simply disappear in the case of popular music, are the central grounds of his criticism in his essays of this time. Adorno characterizes the symphony in terms of its 'incomparably greater density and concision of thematic relationships' (RS 255) than other musical forms. The principle according to which the musical material is arranged is one of repetition and difference: 'If everything in a Beethoven symphony is identical in its ultimate motifical content, nothing is literally identical in the sense of plain repetition, but everything is "different" according to the function it exercises within the development of the whole' (RS 255). The listener in the concert hall, immersed in the sound of the symphony locates each event in relation to the whole. In contrast, a radio broadcast presents discrete events in sequence, focusing attention on single musical details at a time rather than on the form in which they are integrated in relation to the musical whole. The tension and intensity of the relationship between part and whole gives the performance of the symphony a dramatic or dialogic character which is missing from the more narrative version provided by the radio. Rather than being experienced as a process, the symphony becomes a succession of frozen instants. This one-sidedness is not simply the result of reproduction over the airwaves, as Adorno suggests it echoes the Romantic musical turn following Beethoven, of which an emphasis on expressiveness rather than form, and a shift to singular details, were prominent features.

In the case of popular music, which depends on standardized forms, the listener knows what to expect from the beginning of the song: so the details are heard as fitting into a pre-constructed framework, rather than as modifying or negotiating with the structure of the whole piece at every point. In 'serious music', writes Adorno, and for which we can now see that Beethoven provides the definitive example, 'every detail derives its musical sense from the concrete totality of the piece which, in turn, consists of the life relationship of the details and never of a mere enforcement of a musical scheme' (OPM 439). Summing up, Adorno comments: 'the detail virtually contains the whole and leads to the exposition of the whole, while at the same time, it is produced out of the conception of the whole'

(OPM 441). By contrast, in a popular song, the listener should be able to tell at each moment where we are in relation to the whole: this is the end of the verse, the bridge, the chorus. Adorno sees this as being closely linked to the production and distribution of popular music, which depends on a listener being immediately able to place a piece of music, even if they haven't heard it before, in terms of its themes or style. For Adorno's time this would mean the dance style from which the song was derived, but nowadays we would expect to be able to recognize the difference almost instantly between a boy-band's ballad, the sensitive strumming of the singer-songwriter, a raunchy hip-hop track or an alternative rock song. This is why Adorno describes popular music as being like a 'multiple-choice questionnaire' (OPM 446). Record companies may package and sell music in certain ways, but for Adorno popular music has always already pre-packaged itself first.

To this point, Adorno's argument seems to me relatively inoffensive and uncontroversial. He does not deny, for example, that there remains some creativity in the production of a hit song: emphasizing that only the promotion and distribution of popular music can properly be called 'industrial' (OPM 443). Neither can he be accused of simply expressing a preference for non-standardized over standardized music. Indeed, as he had already argued in his 1932 essay 'On the Social Situation of Music', the distinction between music designed specifically for a market, and music which, aspiring to the condition of art, supposedly sets itself against such commercial imperatives, may no longer be valid: 'a great share of supposedly "serious" music adjusts itself to the demands of the market in the same manner as the composers of light music' (EOM 395). Music with artistic pretensions finds itself in the same situation as popular music, which was a commodity all along. Nor does Adorno assume the success of those composers who continue to try and write non-standardized music. *Philosophy of Modern Music* (1949) argues the case somewhat violently for Schoenberg rather than Stravinsky, while in 'The Social Situation of Music' Adorno goes on to discuss at some length the relative success or failure of particular aspects of Schoenberg's work. Adorno's work is primarily critical rather than analytical: he does not aim to catalogue various types of musical work on the basis of an inductive survey of the field, but to assess the 'truth-content' of particular works. Criticism means asking whether a work succeeds.

The difficulty of answering this question becomes a central concern of *Aesthetic Theory*. Adorno's first line reads: 'It is self-evident that nothing concerning art is self-evident anymore, not its inner life, not its relation to the world, not even its right to exist' (AT 1). Or, to sum up Adorno's project in three words: is art possible? Adorno measures contemporary 'serious' or 'art' music against its own claims to be somehow beyond the realm of commerce. The paradox is that any isolation from society may not be a measure of the work's success, but rather the sign of its failure. In his study of the Danish philosopher Søren Kierkegaard, published the following year, Adorno argues that the more one seeks to retreat from the world into isolation or inwardness, the more forcefully the pressure of the outside will remain expressed within that which withdraws.[4] In *Aesthetic Theory*, and throughout his critical writings, he is clear that art's detachment from the world, which distance alone would allow it to take a critical perspective on the way things are, may end up as a kind of consolation for, and affirmation of, the world as it is. With this as his starting point, Adorno undercuts any attempt to establish an automatic hierarchy amongst the different types of music: neither standardized nor non-standardized music has a privileged relationship to critique. Moreover, this distinction makes his treatment of popular music more rather than less even-handed, since he does not judge it against the criteria of an artistic purity it does not claim. (The case of popular music which does make such pretensions we will defer until a later point in the discussion.) That Adorno does decide in favour of non-standardized music is undeniable. But this is based on a further step in his argument which can also explain some of the more controversial aspects of 'On Popular Music'.

The potential difference between standardized and non-standardized music (even if not all 'serious' music achieves this) is that non-standardized music has an intimate connection to the notion of freedom, through seeking autonomy from, rather than submission to, social processes. Adorno's argument in 'On Popular Music' that this cannot be said of standardized music is based on the formal distinction he has drawn between the two types. There is undoubtedly some truth in the suggestion that popular music depends on a certain kind of functionality: on being catchy and appealing in some way. Moreover the industrial distribution of popular music as described by Adorno is based on principles which are still recognizable today, and which underscore its involvement in social life. These include: repetition – saturation coverage is what makes a hit song stand out; a kind of false glamour with which popular music is gilded (but just as 'all glamour girls look alike' [OPM 449] all popular music has to claim the same kinds of glamorous effect); and a tendency towards childish imagery or language. Adorno also refers to journalists who 'need not be bribed' to promote the latest celebrity or event film, however bad it might be, because the economic system has taken precedence over individual preferences and choices. Standardization does not mean rendering everything literally identical – capitalism means a proliferation of competing products – but rather rendering everything of equivalent value, so any choices which remain for the listener are only apparent rather than real ones. It does not matter what so-called artist I prefer, since they are all equally part of the same system. The choices that people believe they make fall into the category of what Adorno calls 'pseudo-individualization': the minor differentiations between the endless repetition of the same product which characterize the output of the culture industry.

Because Adorno is so often and misleadingly accused of being elitist, it is worth reviewing the arguments discussed in this section. It is I hope clear that Adorno does not simply dismiss popular music because of its mass appeal. He is not simply expressing a preference for one type of music rather than another, and then justifying it theoretically. For example, Adorno cannot be said to be simply opting for classical music over popular music, since he is not interested in the repetition of older music, but the production of new music; nor for just any new music which takes its bearings from the European classical tradition; nor is he even sure that there can be successful non-standardized music. Faced by the absorption of both bourgeois art – whose value should derive from its independent critical stance towards society – and of genuinely spontaneous popular culture into processes of production, distribution and reception dominated by the commercial principles of exchange, art may no longer be possible. Adorno judges the appropriate artistic response to be work that goes to great lengths not to fit in, while he is concerned to find appropriate standards by which we might judge such works critically progressive. He states this explicitly in his essay 'On The Fetish Character in Music': 'whether a technique can be considered progressive and "*rational*" depends on this meaning and its place in the whole of society as well as in the organization of the individual work' (EOM 313). He is not interested in shock for the sake of it: shock is a by-product of work which, by responding to its social situation and developing within the framework of a particular musical tradition does something genuinely new, and at odds with prevailing social circumstances. Nothing could be more suspicious to Adorno than a work which simply sets itself against society, and which will always turn out to be the most deeply marked by its social environment.

The differences between what he prefers to call 'standardized' music and 'serious' or 'autonomous' music are only secondarily differences in the production, composition, distribution and performance of the works; and as Adorno observes, these differences are decreasing all the time, as more and more people stop playing music for themselves and depend on commercial middlemen to supply them. More important, indeed decisive, are the differences in the formal aspects of the works. Because Adorno places so much emphasis on the form of the work – on the relationship between the elements in it – he values highly work which requires a certain kind of concentrated attention in order to discern and understand the pattern as it unfolds. What he calls standardized music simply does not make the same demands on the listener: like traditional classical music as distinguished from the work of Schoenberg via the Schumann aphorism cited earlier, it does the listening for you.

What is absolutely essential to grasp, however, is that these are ideal types. Adorno does not simply assume that music which claims to be serious, non-autonomous, non-standardized *is* successful: but that if this is the standard to which it aspires, then it is also that against which it should be judged. Standardized music which makes no claims in these terms must be judged in different ways. The reason Adorno takes this difference so seriously, and can sound so dismissive or patrician when it comes to popular music, is that his insistence on this formal and aesthetic aspect of the music is not a matter of taste, but of establishing the relationship between music and society, between art and freedom. Because he values the possible achievements of art so highly, Adorno has to be brutal about art which he does not believe achieves this standard. To understand more fully what it is that Adorno expects from art, we need to explore a little bit about the aesthetic theories on which he draws.

THE AESTHETICS OF MUSIC

Remembering his first encounter with Ernst Bloch's *The Spirit of Utopia* (1918), which he dates to 1921, Adorno comments that 'the dark brown volume of 400 pages, printed on thick paper, promised something of what one hopes for from medieval books', a promise he had felt as a child from a leather-bound 'eighteenth-century book of magic', a work 'full of abstruse instructions many of which I am still pondering' (NL II 211). If ever there were a book calculated to enchant the young Adorno it would be Bloch's. *The Spirit of Utopia* is a mysterious and arcane writing. Its style is as dense and cryptic as Adorno's mature work, but without some of the professorial apparatus which translates Adorno's thought into the criticism of specific philosophies, books or works of art. At its centre is a reflection on the philosophy of music, drawing together a speculative and visionary account of the interaction between Jewish messianism and Marxist revolutionism. The crisis of meaning diagnosed by so many Weimar intellectuals becomes in Bloch's hand the site of a new beginning, the transition to a better world heralded in the history of music: here taken to be the highest form of art, in line with a tradition which begins in German Romantic philosophy and culminates perhaps in the work of Adorno himself. For the young man struggling to relate his dissatisfaction with the aridity of neo-Kantian philosophizing to his passionate musical involvement, *The Spirit of Utopia* offered both the promise of a reconciliation between these two extremes, in lieu of a more metaphysical transformation, but as Adorno notes, also the lure of falling for a magical solution. That Adorno should be both spellbound by yet deeply suspicious of Bloch's work is symptomatic of his relationship to the aesthetic sphere as such. Rather than assume too quickly that Adorno simply upholds received ideas of the value of high art over debased commercial commodity-music, we need to take some care to reconstruct the outlines of his work on art and culture, and to establish the extent of his inheritance from this aesthetic tradition.

The account of art which Adorno juxtaposes with the commercial world, within whose terms he condemns the descent of the symphony form when strangled and contorted by transmission over the airwaves, and against whose standards he finds popular music lacking, might be characterized in broad terms as Romantic. Specifically, when Adorno discusses art, his ideal model depends on a philosophical account of the place of art and aesthetics which runs through German philosophy from Kant. These days, aesthetics is often considered a rather marginal aspect of philosophy, and our ideas about beauty a mere curiosity for psychological investigation, so it can be hard to grasp how it becomes central to Adorno's account of society and history. This is in part because of the dominance of two ways of thinking about art in contemporary western culture. The first is to treat certain works of art as if they were universally acknowledged to be great. The question asked of a contemporary work of literature, for example, might be 'how does this compare with Shakespeare?' The second is radically opposed to this approach, since it insists that the success of a work of art cannot be universally established, since reactions to art are matters of taste: 'analysis' of art can only revolve around the question 'do I like this?' Neither approach links aesthetic questions to social questions. We might wonder about the possible cohesion of a society in which there is no consensus on such questions as 'what is a successful' work of art, or complain that we live in a culture which no longer produces 'great' works, but these conclusions are inevitable from the shared premises of both approaches: that there is a category of objects which are 'art works' and that the test of their value is the extent of agreement over time about their quality. From this perspective we will always seem to be living in an era whose creative vitality appears to have ebbed away, since our art work can never be as old as that which has come before it, and since our agreement about art tends to be defined by its relative longevity. Adorno's approach puts all these assumptions under scrutiny.

First, it is worth noting that Adorno rarely refers to the idea of 'art' at all. Even in his monumental work *Aesthetic Theory*, he almost always refers to art works, or better still, to a particular art work. This should tell us that he does not believe the idea of 'art' is particularly useful, or that we can take for granted the existence of the category. In other words, the question to be asked when we approach an object which claims to be an art work is: is it art? If the two positions I have sketched might be described as objective and subjective approaches to art, Adorno sits somewhere between the two. This is at least in part due to his reading of Kant. Kant had tried to combine the subjective and objective positions in his account of aesthetic judgement. It was widely acknowledged in eighteenth-century thought that different people have different tastes, but that this in no way invalidates the truth of the statement: 'this is beautiful'. Unlike conceptual, rational knowledge, which must be both objective and universal to be true, the judgement that something is beautiful is subjective, but can still be accepted as universal. In relation to Kant's wider view of the mind, judgements of taste call on our imagination, in ordering our sense perceptions, but not our understanding, since we do not judge something beautiful by recognizing it as fitting under a concept. Put more simply, looking at art is not like doing maths, and even though they are subjective, judgements of taste can be accepted as objectively true. Notice too that, crucially for Adorno, the experience of aesthetics is not conceptual: i.e. it is not wholly amenable to rational, and therefore philosophical, expression.

The German Idealist tradition which develops in the wake of Kant, amidst the turbulent debates over how to interpret his suggestive but elliptical writings, placed a very strong value on the idea of aesthetics. Philosophers like Schelling and Fichte were already dissatisfied with what Adorno and Horkheimer were to describe later as the dialectic of enlightenment. They saw eighteenth-century rationalism as a destructive force, and like Romantic writers more generally, they felt that the idea that the world can be fully described in rational terms led to an impasse. Thinkers of the Enlightenment saw the world as operating in accordance with natural laws, which are the objects of natural science. Believing the operations of the world to be amenable to rational investigation, they enshrined Reason as the arbiter of things. But either reason is itself part of nature, in which case it too is a mechanical force operating according to the laws of nature, and our idea of freedom is an illusion, or we are thrown back onto theological accounts of the world, in which man's autonomy is divinely granted. The solution as the Idealists saw it is that if aesthetics is possible, then man can be shown to make disinterested judgements which are not part of the continuation of natural processes: man is free. Perhaps inevitably, the idea of art and aesthetics becomes central to their idea of philosophy: if their real dissatisfaction is with a wholly rational explanation of the world, art, which appeals to non-rational faculties, seems a natural alternative. As in the work of Schiller, whose *Letters on the Aesthetic Education of Man* read like a more accessible digest of Kant's account, the autonomy of art, its independence from any immediate end or purpose, is of particular importance. Schiller's complaints about the modern world echo those made over a century later by

Adorno: existence in the world is determined by commercial considerations; things are judged solely in terms of their utility; anything which cannot be turned into profit is seen as worthless. Art, however, in the contemplation of which our rational and calculative powers are not engaged, can release us from this mechanistic view of the world.

The extent to which Adorno's understanding of art derives from this Romantic account can be seen in his opposition to directly political art. For Schiller, the improvement of the whole comes as a result of the freedom from ends of its many individuals. Art should be directed first and foremost to engage the disinterested contemplation of the individual, rather than to produce specific political effects or motivations. In his essay on 'Commitment', in part a response to Jean-Paul Sartre's famous call for a political art of engagement in *What Is Literature?*, Adorno echoes the Romantic position. For Adorno art does not become political by virtue of discussing or representing political problems directly, but by virtue of its form. In his essay Adorno clarifies Sartre's argument – that he is not asking for political propaganda, but for an art which provokes us to take a decisive attitude on matters of principle – and admits to a certain sympathy with this line. But he suggests that the horrified response of the human being to torture is not to be elicited by confronting them with torture on stage. Rather it is to be extracted from the relationships and dynamics within the construction of the artistic material itself. This means a work of art which can no longer take for granted the possibility of art: in the face of extremity, art becomes self-critical, as if tearing itself apart in the face of the awful reality of a world in which genocide, nuclear destruction and man's inhumanity are so evident. Sartre's mistake is twofold: a political naïvety or miscalculation, in so far as there is always a risk that art will dignify and bestow a glamour on what it represents, will cloak truth with untruth; and a conceptual misunderstanding of what art is. Art, for Adorno, is a function of those elements of a work which are not consumed in communication, in the transmission of a message. It is not perhaps insignificant that Sartre and Adorno are both involved in the production of art. But Sartre is a writer, and for Adorno literature always has a questionable status in relationship to art, since it is so heavily burdened with language, which itself threatens to turn into mere communication. For Adorno the musician and composer, as for the German Romantic tradition of which he is the belated heir, music is the higher form, because further from communication of a particular message.

We sometimes distinguish between the form of a work of art and its content. This may well be because we base our ideas of art on literature or painting, in which it is apparently quite easy to separate out what is represented within the work from the style in which this is done. If abstract painting or experimental poetry seem to turn the style of the work into its subject matter, forcing us to think about how we perceive and represent things, this is a relatively minor diversion from the essentially representational and communicative function of these forms. But Adorno begins from music, which has always been the least representational, least able to imitate something in the world. Once music began to be increasingly separated from words or from any immediate social function such as accompanying dancing, in the Romantic period, it was widely considered the highest form of art for precisely this reason. So the distinction between form and content is not of much use for Adorno: an art work is not primarily a representation of something, but a set of formal relations. The material of which it is composed may in part point outwards to the world, but it will also include formal elements which link back to earlier art. The 'message' or 'point' of a work of art, if we can still speak of such things, consists in its negotiation of these relationships, rather than in some 'meaning' which can be detached and taken away from it.

To conclude this section, we might say that one aspect of Adorno's work amounts to an affirmation of this Romantic aesthetic tradition, which is primarily formalist. All his analyses treat works of art as complex composites of various material elements: these elements would include not only the artistic materials (particular pigments, notes, words) from which the work is constructed, its thematic subject matter, or the object depicted, where appropriate, but also the principles of composition, some kind of negotiation with preceding artistic forms, and some idea of the society against which the art work sets itself, but which leaves its mark on the art work nonetheless. Unlike most Romantic theories of art, Adorno does not privilege the unity of the whole over its elements: 'what crackles in art works is the sound of the friction of the antagonistic elements that the art work seeks to unify' (AT 177). Since works exist in time, the relationships between these elements are not static but variable. Criticism will never be completed, since an art work is itself never finished as its elements transform in time. In focusing so intently on

the art work itself, Adorno resolutely opposes other theories of interpretation which judge art in terms of the intentions of the artist, or
its reception by an audience. Even if we could finally secure knowledge of either, we would be no nearer an understanding of the art
work as an object. The case of historical theories of art is more
complex, as we shall see: where Adorno departs from the Romantic
tradition is in accepting that, just as we saw with the idea of culture
in the previous chapter, these ideas about art have a history, and the
fact of their historicity opens up another perspective on them.
Adorno strives to treat art from both directions at once, which puts
him at once within and beyond the aesthetic tradition.

MODERNISM OR AVANT-GARDE?

Inevitably, Adorno's thinking on art is bound up with the artistic
production of his age. Not the abstract possibility of art but only its
concrete existence would prove that there is freedom in the world, so
Adorno's account of art must develop in tandem with his responses
to particular artworks. Since I am concerned above all to outline the
principles of Adorno's work, since only the form of his thought, not
its particular contents, can provide us with the basis for our own
judgements, I will not devote much time to those artists whom
Adorno particularly admired. Instead I will draw on what has become
a conventional distinction in cultural history between modernist and
avant-garde art to characterize Adorno's position. Although strictly
speaking it is anachronistic to discuss Adorno's work in the context
of this distinction, since it is not one he uses in his work, I believe it
is useful because it highlights the continued relevance of his thought:
the common currency of the contrast between avant-garde and modernism is evidence of a confusion about the relationship between
politics and art into which Adorno is never tempted.

The distinction arises in an attempt to clarify the relationships
between politics, society and art in the early twentieth century. Both
modernism and the avant-garde are said to share a common concern
to 'make it new', in Ezra Pound's phrase: to engage in a criticism of
society through the production of works of art which exploit formal
dissonance and shock to fracture and disconcert perceptions of the
integrity of reality. However, the avant-garde is distinguished from
modernism on the ground that the Surrealists and Dadaists, extended
art's critical dimension into an interrogation of the relationship

between art and society, up to the point of attacking the idea of artistic autonomy on which the critical distance of modernism from the social world rests. The need for such a distinction is largely political: it enables critics in the second half of the twentieth century to differentiate between what they think of as progressive and reactionary strains within the artistic movements of the first half. However, it also responds to a historical necessity. Modernism in general declared itself to be an emancipation from Romanticism; but subsequent critics with less personal investment in making a break with the past have pointed out that in many ways it could be seen as a continuation of Romantic doctrines. Meanwhile, other readers of Romanticism have shown the earlier movement to be far less affirmative, and far more critical, than had been previously assumed. The idea of the avant-garde could serve to identify those modernists who did succeed in making a break with Romanticism, by distinguishing modernism into those tendencies which continue the aesthetic tradition, and those which sought to make a break with it.

Adorno is hard to situate in relation to such a distinction. His insistence on formal criticism relates him in very broad terms to the formalism shared by modernism understood in its widest sense. His advocacy of a composer like Schoenberg links him fairly obviously to late Romanticism: as we have seen, Adorno insists that the value of Schoenberg is that what may be a fairly radical transformation is still broadly related to the tradition that precedes it. Schoenberg's experimentation is led by the musical material itself, rather than being imposed on it in an attempt to challenge the relationship between the composer and his audience: it represents an attempt to perfect or complete the Romantic aesthetic tradition of autonomous art rather than to displace or destroy it. But on the other hand, Adorno can be seen to turn against the idea of autonomous art itself, when he suggests not only that autonomous art may no longer be possible, but that it has always been compromised, too strongly stamped by its supposed opposition to society to do anything other than conform to social demands. As a consequence Adorno shares a great deal of common ground with the avant-garde criticism of the institutionalization of art. For example, both associate the museum with the mausoleum: they 'are like the family sepulchres of works of art. They testify to the neutralization of culture' (P 175).

There are two reasons for difficulty of placing Adorno in relation to the distinction between modernism and the avant-garde. The first is that Adorno's cultural criticism depends on an alternation between examining its object from within and from without culture. Adorno accepts that the aesthetic tradition of autonomous art is itself historical. 'What are taken to be the purest forms (e.g. traditional musical forms) can be traced back even in the smallest idiomatic detail to content such as dances' (AT 5): the idea of art depends on a historical repression of the social use of artistic forms. The emancipation of art from religious or social functions is a form of denial or forgetting which means that the 'immanent historicity' of artworks is 'a dialectic of nature and its domination' (AT 5). Like all cultural products, art works bear within them the traces of the destruction of nature by reason, and the domination of the whole over the particular, which characterize the development of capitalist society since the eighteenth century. The purported autonomy of art has already been compromised from the beginning. If we accept for the moment the distinction between the modernist, who wishes to emancipate society through culture, and the avant-gardist, who wishes to destroy culture in order to emancipate society, we would have to say that Adorno does not easily fit either position. Like the avant-garde, Adorno has had enough of culture, and seeks new powers of creation through its destruction; but like the modernist, he is not quite ready to throw off culture yet. Since I am not convinced that such a distinction can be usefully sustained, it does not seem urgent to me to judge Adorno as either one thing or the other, modernist or avant-garde. The point of the discussion is to emphasize the essentially ambivalent nature of Adorno's relationship to the aesthetic tradition.

The issues at stake here can be clarified by locating Adorno in relation to other Marxist theories of art. The predominant orthodox approach has been to see art in purely instrumental terms: art should depict the truth of the political situation in order to persuade people of the need to act, or it should show an ideal situation in order to inspire them. A more modernist approach, such as that of Brecht, sees art not as representation, but in terms of shock effect: by disturbing conventional relationships between audience and performance, as well as by disrupting conventional narrative techniques, Brecht seeks to bypass the conformism which threatens autonomous art. Ultimately, however, Brecht's work is intended to spur action. In doing so, it already transgresses the aesthetic principle that art should be disinterested. By contrast, the art in which Adorno is interested is that which it would be hardest to integrate into the commodity process. It is disruptive, problematic. This does not simply mean that it should be unlistenable or offensive. Like Schoenberg's music, it may seem difficult because it confronts its own relationship with tradition, and seeks to break free from established conventions, but Adorno's idea of extreme art is not simply an art of excess, or of obscenity.

An art which simply reacted to social values or expectations would be its inverted mirror image, and would confirm on the one hand society's sense of its own superiority, and on the other the artist's illusion of independence and freedom. The avant-garde claim to have seen through social illusion risks inventing a true world and a false world, one of the fundamental illusions of metaphysics for both Nietzsche and Adorno. A successful work of art is one which questions rather than confirms the opposition between art and society, by showing art's autonomy to be an illusion. Paradoxically, such a work would affirm the possibility of autonomy. Art must become self-critical, it must negotiate with the idea of art itself, rather than simply turning against it: 'In the face of the abnormality into which reality is developing, art's inescapable affirmative essence has become insufferable. Art must turn against itself, in opposition to its own concept, and thus become uncertain of itself right into its innermost fiber' (AT 2). What Adorno calls dissonance is the effect of this self-criticism in art: it depends on maintaining a critical relation to the aesthetic tradition, rather than rejecting it in the name of something else. As we shall see in the next section, this is because we can only ever be in culture: the claim to have reached an outside is illusory.

We are now in a position to see why the charge of elitism might resurface in relation to Adorno's idea of art. Because its success depends to such a great extent on a negotiation with traditional western art, for anyone not versed in this tradition it may make little sense. But given Adorno's premises, this difficulty is unavoidable. Art is not critical by virtue of its relationship to society, since its relationship to society is what compromises its autonomy. Rather, art is critical by virtue of its critical relationship to other art, to tradition, and through the structural relationships between the materials of which it is composed. While Adorno shares the widely felt avant-garde concern with the decay of language and experience in the modern world and the need to invigorate or renew through shock, he recognizes that the shock must be mediated rather than immediate. A critical response to art requires considerable analysis and a certain amount of background knowledge. If we balk at this exacting demand, we should remember that it owes in part to a sense of the corruption of the Romantic aesthetic tradition which promises to overcome rational reflection and political division through the harmony of taste and feeling. As throughout Adorno's work, its political thrust passes through the bourgeois individualism which it seeks to destroy, in the belief that any attempt to short-circuit the rational self-critique of reason will be a reversion to irrationalism.

Adorno acknowledges the need for musical education as a prerequisite of criticism in an essay on 'new' music: it shocks because it deviates from what 'for the majority of people' are 'fixed notions as to what constitutes music', owing 'to their experiences ever since their early childhood, their education and the overwhelming predominance of everything that inundates them in the name of music' (QF 251). Adorno's interest in the NBC *Music Appreciation Hour* is precisely that it promises to offer such an education in music; his dissatisfaction comes from the fact that it does not treat art the way he views it, and simply presents a list of 'great composers' and teaches people how to recognize their work. In other words it assumes that there is such a thing as great art, which people can be taught to identify. But this is absolutely counter to Adorno's view: the importance of aesthetic experience is that it is subjective. If art is possible, I am free when I contemplate it, and this will help overcome the prevailing unfreedom of the contemporary world. But this depends on me making a judgement of my own, rather than simply expressing an opinion or taking on trust that such and such a work is art. I must constantly ask not 'is this great art?' or 'do I like it?' but 'is this even art?'.

In this section I have tried to emphasize that Adorno approaches the traditional claims made for a link between art and freedom from two directions. On the one hand, he seems to be squarely situated within the German Idealist or Romantic tradition, suggesting that art, by virtue of its relative autonomy from the material processes of production and consumption in the commercial world, has a privileged relation to critique. On the other hand, where in the aesthetic tradition the individual's disinterested contemplation of art is a step towards a reconciled world, Adorno is rather more circumspect, and it is art criticism, rather than art appreciation, which might draw out the work's 'truth-content' and emancipatory potential. Criticism only follows or matches a process of self-criticism which already takes place in the art work itself, which must call into question its own relationship to the concept of art. The apparent refutation of aesthetics by experience – the failure of art to lead to a reconciled world in the face of capitalism – cannot of itself be enough to expose this tradition as a fraud: art might still be possible, just rare. Adorno's aim therefore has to be to write from a standpoint both within that tradition, continuing to pose its own questions, and outside it, exposing it to the challenge of everyday life in the modern world, at the same time. The world can still be judged against the aesthetic ideal, and found wanting; but the grounds of the aesthetic ideal itself may also be brought into question. The possibility of freedom is only ever at stake when our thinking about art achieves such a dialectical and self-critical standpoint.

HISTORY AND TRUTH-CONTENT

To summarize the argument so far: although Adorno is firmly committed to the understanding of art which comes down to him from the Idealist tradition, he is extremely critical of most of what passes for art in modern bourgeois life. What makes art important – its resistance to conceptual or rational determination – makes it the perfect ideological counterpart to everyday life in capitalist society: 'industry makes even this resistance an institution and changes it into coin' (AT 336). Not only Adorno's idea of what constitutes an aesthetic theory – reflection on the very possibility of art today, but any attempt to think about art 'disturbs the weekend pleasures to which art has been consigned as the complement to bourgeois routine' (AT 335). But while we may not be surprised that a large part of Adorno's work on art and culture is devoted to showing the failure of most works that aspire to the status of art to achieve autonomy it is perhaps harder to see why he should also have approving words for what in 'On Popular Music' he calls standardized music.

In a short essay simply entitled 'Kitsch', Adorno defends what he calls 'good bad music', music which does not claim to be part of the progressive tradition of art but still retains a certain value (EOM 502), distinguishing it from 'bad good music', art works which have failed (EOM 502). Kitsch is for Adorno a bit like a museum of past musical forms, 'things that were part of the art of a former time and are undertaken today' (EOM 501); but it also embraces the process of standardization: it is specifically 'constructed in types' and 'as soon as a new type turns up . . . a large group of similar compositions is created . . .;

or a type emerges in innumerable examples simultaneously' (EOM 503). Adorno does object to what he calls 'kitsch with "class"', kitsch with pretensions to artistic sophistication, much as he objects to any supposed art which does not push towards extremes: as ever his criticism seems to be mostly aimed at the comfortable middle-ground where something claims to be artistic without challenging convention. Indeed he is concerned that attacks on kitsch have become a way of defending 'a "moderate" culture of the musical that no longer possesses any power' (EOM 504).

Despite Adorno's reputation as an elitist, it is much easier to make sense of his account of art and culture, and his specific version of the task of criticism if we begin at the point where both bourgeois art and popular culture may testify to something better, but in which neither can escape domination by the commercial world. Adorno's refusal to reject kitsch out of hand demonstrates two crucial points. Firstly, that he does not only allow a critical content to autonomous art, i.e. art constructed in accord with the principles of the German aesthetic tradition to which he stands in complex relation. Secondly, that his conception of art and culture is intrinsically historical. Kitsch may be made from out-of-date art, but this alerts us to the essential historicity of all art. Adorno stresses this again and again in *Aesthetic Theory*: 'important art works constantly divulge new layers; they age, grow cold, and die' (AT 4). Their critical relationship to society must also be variable. Indeed, Adorno suggests that great art works might come in and go out of phase with society: at points their critical potential will be stilled; at others it will be alive and vivid. There will always remain something critical in the art work: 'Authentic art of the past that for the time being must remain veiled is not thereby sentenced. Great works wait . . . something of their truth content, however little it can be pinned down, does not: it is that whereby they remain eloquent' (AT 40).

Adorno's 1957 essay 'The Aging of the New Music' addresses this question directly, reflecting on such a process in action. How can it be that the work of the Schoenberg school, and of his beloved and respected composition teacher Alban Berg, has been surrendered to the 'aficionados of modernism' (EOM 182)? Its 'critical impulse is ebbing away' (EOM 181). Adorno gives two answers: one, highly technical, examines the specific history of the reactions to Schoenberg's musical innovations, which saw his ideas degraded into that of a methodology by 'tone-row engineers' (EOM 198), used to churn out imitations or replicas, without the same tension between system and expression which characterized his own music. The second is more complex: this is the need to think history and art together. Society has become more rationalized, and conversely truly autonomous art has been driven further and further out of sight: 'the only authentic art works produced today are those that in their inner organization measure themselves by the fullest experience of horror, and there is scarcely anyone, except Schoenberg or Picasso, who can depend on himself to have the power to do this' (EOM 200). Such claims appear to go against what I have suggested earlier is Adorno's hesitation about ascribing some kind of historical 'end' to art: in which case our appreciation of his strategy here must depend on our evaluation of statements like: 'nobody really believes in "culture" anymore' (EOM 200). The distinction between art and kitsch shows us that art can fail, there can be bad good art. But does Adorno go on to introduce a historical argument which dictates that such failure is more likely today? To see how this works, we need to reconsider the central category of Adorno's own version of art criticism: 'truth-content'.

Adorno's understanding of 'truth-content' is what enables him to stand both inside and outside the aesthetic and critical tradition he inherits, and therefore to sustain its criticism of the modern world while also threatening to expose its own blind spots. It is also closely linked to his insistence on the importance of history. Like many of the art works he valued most highly, which challenge the idea of art itself, and therefore look unfamiliar or strange when held up to traditional accounts of artistic achievement, Adorno's work does not fit comfortably into any of the critical paradigms with which we are most familiar. In particular his distinctive – and distinctly obscure – combination of formal analysis of the material construction of the art work with a strong emphasis on the historical dimension of art squats somewhat uneasily athwart the two dominant strands of modern criticism, which tend to focus on either one or the other. For the formalist critic, the possibility of art is simply a given, indeed his claim to authority rests on the ability to identify and discriminate between works of art. The effects of art are the product of the interplay between the formal elements of the work: any disagreement with which the formalist's pronouncements might be greeted are the product of insufficient training on the part of the hostile observer. For a historicist on the other hand, ideas about art are relative to particular cultural contexts. There is no inherent worth to a work of art, and no reason why someone from one cultural background should judge as valuable an art work from another cultural background. In this case the definition of the art work is variable.

Adorno shares elements with both positions, while managing to refute both. It's a neat trick, but the result is an uncomfortable balancing act for the philosopher. Adorno emphasizes that art should be understood in formal terms, rather than representational ones. In other words, the central question, as we saw in his response to Sartre, is not what a work of art depicts (already a deeply ambiguous question in relation to music) but the relationship between the whole and its parts, and how the particular work's structure is related to that of other works: its negotiation with tradition. Yet Adorno also emphasizes that art is historical through and through, that all the elements from which a work is constructed are social and historical. Art is not a path to another realm of existence, and all its materials are primarily of this world. From the first position, Adorno's insistence on the historical variability of the 'truth-content' of the art work looks like a variant of the second: it will appear as if Adorno sees art as simply relative to a specific context. There is certainly evidence in Adorno's work to support this view, particularly the genealogical assumption that high art develops in conjunction with the political and social triumph of the bourgeois against the *ancien régime* in Europe, and their subsequent need to suppress working-class rebellion. However from the second position, Adorno's insistence on 'truth' itself may seem problematic. If Adorno believes there is something called art which can be distinguished by its truth, he is an ignorant formalist; but in his rejection of the idea that art is a cultural phenomenon – i.e. that there is high art – and low art, and both are equally 'valid' or 'true' – he looks like an elitist proponent of the second position.

'Truth-content' is the tricky category which somehow bridges these two positions, but cannot be identified from either. It is what Adorno's aesthetics really rests on. It is particularly unfortunate that it is such an obscure concept in his writing. As in the discussion of new music, an art work's 'truth' is its critical content, an indication of its success in setting itself against society (which defines art in the aesthetic tradition). This truth is always historically variable, and may be assimilated by society – the culture industry – or emerge from it as times change. But Adorno gives little more indication of what 'truth-content' is than that. In fact, the definition of 'truth-content' emerges in negative terms, as being neither one thing nor the other, rather than in positive ones: this is because any system or methodology of criticism would become complicit in the dissolution of art in society. For example:

> Aesthetics is under no obligation to deduce the objectivity of its historical content in historicizing fashion, as being the inevitable result of the course of history; rather, this objectivity is to be grasped according to the form of that historical content. It is not, as the trivial paradigm would have it, that aesthetics moves and is transformed in history: History is immanent to the truth content of aesthetics. (AT 357)

If for the formalist a work is true, or not, and for the historicist a work's truth is understood as the historical forces which have given it shape, for Adorno 'truth-content' is more like the work's achievement of a temporary and revocable autonomy against social forces. This autonomy requires criticism to release it. Art and popular culture give us access to the memory or promise of freedom from the overbearing totality of society, but cannot in themselves be said to set us free. In practice, it has to be said, Adorno's criticism can look reductive, since the negative truth of a successful work of art is always that of the dialectic of freedom, autonomy and society, as each participates in and challenges the same whole.

One possible criticism of Adorno that is worth considering here – because it illuminates very clearly his objectives – is the idea that this is simply not what art is all about. As we have seen, the Romantic account of art privileges the idea that it gives access to a non-conceptual 'truth': an instinctive or vital tapping into some aspect of existence which rational thought cannot achieve. In some washed-out form this remains a typical claim of a naïve account of art: art is simply the inspired creation of artists, and it moves us. Adorno's critical and rationalist approach to the art work, which demands that the viewer break down the work into its formal elements and appreciate their structural relations, and approaches evaluation by contesting the art's claim to autonomy, is anathema to this idea of art. However in *Aesthetic Theory* Adorno defends himself at some length against such charges. Broadly, Adorno's arguments are twofold: that this idea of the irrational 'authenticity' of art is precisely that aspect of it which is most fully exploited by commercial society, which seeks to sell us the illusion of 'nature', of relief or escape from the demands of every-day existence; and that this kind of critical approach does not contravene the work of the artist, but repeats it. An art work, Adorno suggests, is always already critical: it is inherently a negotiation with the tradition, with other art works, and thus implicitly evaluation or commentary on the conceptual material. Treating the art seriously is not to betray the work of art, but to treat it with the respect it deserves.

What Adorno particularly loathes is the middle ground between kitsch and autonomous art. Because of its dialectical structure, Adorno's thought tends to extremes, and this can clearly be seen in his analysis of art and culture. The idea of autonomous art, however degraded in practice, keeps alive a memory of the promise of freedom. The question of the products of the culture industry is related but slightly different: Adorno uncovers traces of a popular culture which could not be assimilated into capitalism. In neither case can we simply point to successful resistance to capitalism, but neither art nor kitsch can be dismissed out of hand as *wholly* commodified. This seems to be confirmed from another remark in his letter to Benjamin. Adorno suggests that both the great work of art and the cinema 'bear the stigmata of capitalism, both contain elements of change (but never of course the middle-term between Schoenberg and the American film). Both are torn halves of an integral freedom, to which however they do not add up'.[5] The implication seems to be that either the highest or the lowest art (in shorthand terms, but Adorno would probably clarify this as autonomous art and mass-produced art) contain more possibilities for freedom than the middlebrow. We should be careful of implying one term where another is used, but it is certainly the case that for Adorno it is the middle ground of culture which is the problem: and in particular, mass-produced art which aspires to be taken more seriously than it deserves, or autonomous art which resigns its autonomy in being consigned to mass reproduction.

Although his friend Walter Benjamin is himself an esoteric and complex thinker, a comparison can help us understand three aspects of Adorno's work. Firstly, Adorno seems to have absorbed more than a little of Benjamin's nominalism, a stubborn belief that the tiniest fragment is somehow more 'true' than the whole. This is anti-systematic and somewhat anarchic. Secondly, we might understand Adorno's idea of 'truth-content' as referring to the absolutely singular and specific aspect of a work, that which makes it unique and which resists any appropriation within a larger category, such as a particular generic form, or the product of a particular artist, or technical process. In his 'Theses on the Philosophy of History' Benjamin comments that 'the past carries with it a temporal index by which it is referred to redemption', and that 'the past can be seized only as an image which flashes up at the instant when it can be recognized and is never seen again'.[6] Only the radical specificity and uniqueness of each fragment of the world, dispersed in space and time, holds the power to resist the totality of the system. For Benjamin and Adorno these particulars resist conceptual thought, so cannot be identified, but the task of criticism is nevertheless to seek to recognize them. Perhaps we could understand this as the attempt to identify the moment at which a particular work comes into a particular configuration with the world as a whole which lends it a critical charge. But as soon as it has been reported, such critical potential has dissipated, just as the critical account becomes part of the culture industry rather than standing in opposition to it.

This seems to me the central lesson of Adorno's criticism: something like a principle of allowing the object to survive, allowing the possibility of right life to continue, allowing for hope of freedom, without stopping, bringing to a halt or freezing the dialectical historical process. It is clearly expressed in the following remark taken from Adorno's essay on Georg Lukács:

> The substantive content of a work of art can survive in the precise, wordless polemic which depicts the dawn of a nonsensical world; and it can vanish again as soon as it is positively asserted, as soon as existence is claimed for it, a fate similar to that which befalls the didactic antithesis between a right and a wrong mode of life to be found in Tolstoy after *Anna Karenina*.[7]

The substantive, i.e. the true, content of a work of art stems from its antagonism to the world. But as soon as we label, identify or claim to know such a content, we abolish it, and thus the critical value of the work. In the next chapter we will move on to examine the question of freedom and morality introduced here. Just as claiming to distinguish true from false art inevitably turns the true into the false by subsuming it to a larger social purpose, so the claim to know how to live 'rightly' will turn out to be the moment at which the possibility of morality is betrayed.

THE CULTURE INDUSTRY

'The culture industry' is a phrase introduced to Adorno's work in the essay 'Enlightenment as Mass Deception', which he co-wrote with Max Horkheimer in *Dialectic of Enlightenment*. It has come to be almost synonymous with Adorno's views, which is unfortunate since it can be easily misunderstood. We can get a flavour of this problem by considering Adorno and Horkheimer's comments on the state of animation in the early 1940s: 'cartoon and stunt films were once exponents of fantasy against rationalism. They allowed justice to be done to the animals and things electrified by their technology, by granting the mutilated beings a second life. Today they merely confirm the victory of technological reason over truth' (DE 110). By abolishing any semblance of plot in favour of a repetitive formula in which the only surprise is the form that the violence inflicted on the characters will take, cartoons have become 'organized cruelty' (the 1944 edition has 'lust for murder'). Adorno and Horkheimer's conclusion seems almost hysterical: 'To the extent that cartoons do more than accustom the senses to the new tempo, they hammer into every brain the old lesson that continuous attrition, the breaking of all individual resistance, is the condition of life in this society. Donald Duck in the cartoons and the unfortunate victim in real life receive their beatings so that the spectators can accustom themselves to theirs' (DE 110). Comments such as these have led unsympathetic and hasty readers to conclude that Adorno and Horkheimer simply oppose all popular culture as such, on the grounds that it coerces its audience into consent with the state of society as it is. This has been seen as elitist, since it looks as if it privileges the culture of one class over the culture of another. However, this is not quite what they are arguing; while the grounds of the opposition to this supposed elitism reveals a lot about the importance of their argument.

In the context of Adorno's work as a whole, we should be able to see that 'the culture industry' is a sort of nickname for the situation which we have already described: in which art, whose autonomy and critical power derive from its opposition to society, may no longer be possible since it has proved easy to assimilate to the commercial world; while other cultural forms make no such critical claim. If art were indeed the property of a particular class, this argument would be the narrative of a decline: of art's contamination by contact with the commercial world, and the freedom to which art gives access would be reserved for those who can afford to remain uncontaminated by commerce. However, the tradition on which Adorno draws makes no such assumption: art is in principle universal, i.e. available to everyone, although in fact considerations such as available leisure time, wealth and access to museums, galleries and concert halls might in fact limit art's universality. Given its Kantian roots, this tradition's claims for art only make sense if they are rooted in a universal human ability: art's link to freedom and spontaneity depends on a particular understanding of human nature. Adorno turns against the tradition in showing that 'art' is not a universal human capacity, but rather associated with the rise of the bourgeoisie in the eighteenth century. But if the factual origins of modern art are bourgeois, this does not mean that it is in principle restricted to the bourgeoisie. Moreover, the idea of the culture industry is a shorthand way of saying that these claims for aesthetic freedom fail anyway, as if the bourgeois have only managed to create pretty pictures to adorn the walls of the prison cell they have built themselves.

Critics of Adorno, and of the bourgeois conception of art in general, have tended to uphold the idea of working-class culture as somehow spontaneous and authentic. From this point of view the analysis of the culture industry is specifically designed to show that the art consumed by the mass of the population is nothing of the sort, and to deny a full humanity to the people. What they fail to see is that while Adorno attacks the idea that the effect of art is of a spontaneous and immediate beauty – 'Art without reflection is the retrospective fantasy of a reflexive age' (AT 337) – he also attacks the idea that there is something 'free' or 'authentic' about working-class culture. Like 'art without reflection' such freedom could only ever be a fantasy: it will always be mediated by the culture industry. Looking back on his and Horkheimer's arguments in their earlier essay together, he remarks: 'In our drafts we spoke of "mass culture". We replaced that expression with "culture industry" in order to exclude from the outset the interpretation agreeable to its advocates: that it is a matter of something like a culture that arises spontaneously from the masses themselves, the contemporary form of popular art' (CI 98). Note that Adorno does not deny the possibility of a genuine art form that does not belong to the bourgeois aesthetic tradition ('popular art') but rather its possibility today. This is the same challenge he levels at autonomous art. Just as it would be up to the defenders of high culture to prove that a work has somehow escaped

the trammels of the culture industry, so it would be up to the sup-
porter of popular culture to demonstrate its spontaneity.

It is essential to grasp the fact that when Adorno uses the phrase
'culture industry' he does not mean it to be synonymous with 'entertainment industry', and his criticisms of it are not just based on the
complaint that it seems to have swallowed up autonomous art.
Adorno is concerned with culture as a whole. The idea of industry is
added to qualify the term culture and to indicate that this situation is
neither natural, nor inevitable, nor spontaneous. The entertainment
industry which Adorno and Horkheimer were able to observe close at
hand in their Californian years comes to serve as a metaphor for what
has happened to the very idea of culture. Since our imagination of
something 'outside' the culture industry will inevitably be marked by
the culture industry, so we cannot simply oppose anything to it as
somehow 'truer' or more 'free'. Least of all can we argue that popular
culture, whether the product of the entertainment industry or not,
is 'free' or 'authentic' since one of the hallmarks of the culture industry's rationalization of our ways of thinking is to embrace anything
'spontaneous', 'irrational' or 'creative' and present it as a valuable
alternative or supplement to its own rational processes. Adorno and
Horkheimer's use of the phrase 'the culture industry' is an attempt to
find a vocabulary with which they can outflank the two intertwined
positions which they oppose: the bourgeois disdain for popular
culture which fails to become art; and the polemical dismissal of art
as simply false. If freedom is linked to art, either argument abolishes
freedom, the former by being unable to acknowledge its own imbri-
cation with historical and social forces, the latter by doing away with
art and therefore criticism altogether.

Part of the problem here stems from the ambiguities of the term
'culture'. Although German has two words, *kultur* and *bildung*, where
English only has one, this is of little help in clarifying the situation. In
both languages a range of meanings overlap, but there are two dominant and conflicting uses. The first is a remnant of the term's original derivation from the idea of growth and cultivation, a sense it
retains in words like 'agriculture'. Used in this sense, culture means
something like education or development: this is a normative term,
and expresses approval, for example when we describe someone as
'cultured'. From this the term has come to designate aspects of social
life such as art or philosophy which, taken as evidence of development
imply something better than either entertainment or mere opinion.

The second use of the term is much more common nowadays and protests against the first use: 'culture' in this sense implies the sum total of the behaviours, beliefs and practices common to a specific group of people, with no hierarchical distinctions being drawn between different activities. This relativism is directly implied when we refer to different national or ethnic 'cultures', implying equally valid ways of life. In the first case we oppose 'culture' to that which is without culture; in the second we oppose one culture to another. What the German word *bildung* does illuminate is the sense in which culture can be closely linked to the idea of education or improvement. So when Adorno complains about a decline of culture, we need to try and work out whether he means the decline of a specific set of practices, for example the Idealist conception of art, in the context of the beliefs of society as a whole, or whether he means that society as such can no longer be considered progressive.

Throughout the twentieth century the second meaning of the term gained ground on the first, as it has become less acceptable to seem to make judgements on grounds of quality. In the context of this debate, Adorno looks as if he is taking the (perfectly respectable but unpopular) position that high culture is more worthwhile than popular culture. But if Adorno means the second, then the culture of society as a whole is declining. Adorno's position is somewhat ambiguous, as he often switches rapidly between the two meanings of the word, and his readers in English have to try to second-guess a distinction often left silent by translators. However, this ambiguity need not be debilitating, once we grasp it as essential to Adorno's understanding of the position of the cultural critic. Because Adorno is no longer confident in the saving power of 'high' culture, he is critical of it; however, he also notices that those elements in it which might still do some good are increasingly less characteristic of society as a whole, in which case culture itself might be said to be in decline. Because only those elements of high culture offer criteria by which we might judge the progress or otherwise of a society, to give up on high culture also means to give up on the idea of progress as such. Twentieth-century intellectuals of both the left and right have been insistent on the value of high culture for precisely this reason and have often believed that exposure of the majority of the population to 'high' culture will somehow improve the culture of everyone: this is the Idealist legacy at work. Adorno's more ambivalent position is that due to the corruption of high culture, it may not even have anything to offer society. Part of his polemical target is the idea that it is possible to 'educate' the masses through their exposure to so-called high culture via the mass media; and it is perhaps not surprising that in his essay 'The Theory of Pseudo-Culture' Adorno reserves his greatest vitriol for a book which claims to introduce you to great music by teaching you to recognize select motifs from specific symphonies.

In fact 'The Theory of Pseudo-Culture' offers a relatively clear account of Adorno's position. What is particularly important to stress is that for the most part he emphasizes that culture is not 'high' culture, but something more like our entire ways of doing things in a society. The triumph of pseudo-culture is the victory of what claims to offer an improved society, but fails to. In other words, for a society to be only pseudo-cultured is for it to have failed to mature, develop or progress. The German word translated as 'pseudo-culture' makes this clearer: *halbbildung* could also be translated as 'half-educated'. So 'the culture industry' is a way of abstracting those social forces which have led to this situation, and which threaten the possibility of either bourgeois or popular art. In his lectures on sociology Adorno remarks that in this phrase 'should be included all the powers of social integration in a wider sense'.[8] But since these forces would include all our ways of thinking, feeling and acting, but particularly our philosophical reasoning or historical understanding, we are actually dealing with a rather complex epistemological puzzle. Caught within culture, which has failed to live up to its promise of delivering a social world which is not dominated by violence, oppression and exploitation, we have no means other than those of culture by which we might diagnose and seek to resolve the situation. In many ways this is the central problem with which Adorno's work as a whole is concerned, and it accounts for his insistence on the need to be self-critical. Since the only set of tools we have is compromised, we need to be as subtle, as careful and as circumspect about how we use them, and always undertaking to accept the possibility that they will do more harm than good.

The importance of understanding this as an epistemological problem as well as a historical one needs also to be stressed. Because our idea of history is deeply bound to that of culture (we think of cultures as having histories; we understand history in terms of the progression and development of culture; our idea of what 'objective' history is must be influenced by the cultural context of our thought), we cannot simply look for a historical remedy to this situation. A revolution would need to be a revolution of thought as much as a social one. This means that the possibility of genuine progress cannot be presumed: and Adorno's own relentless work of criticism implies that the negation or refutation of every movement which claims to be progress is preferable to embracing and affirming particular forms of social or cultural resistance.

So when we encounter elements in Adorno's work which do counter the total domination of the culture industry, the priority of the whole over the individual and the creation of false needs, we should be slightly cautious about assuming that he has, for example, changed his mind about the possibility of progress. Certainly there is some evidence that in later years Adorno may have found the results of empirical research into social attitudes rather more optimistic than he had anticipated. Comments in the final lecture of his *Introduction to Sociology* course (11 July 1968), and in the late essay on 'Free Time' (1969) (CM 174–5) suggest he has. Adorno realizes that the reverence of people for the celebrities whose images surround them may be far less than he has previously allowed: 'what is drummed into [people] as essential to society . . . is not in reality as remotely as relevant as it claimed to be'.[9] The attraction of the idea that changes his mind is that it reintroduces a redemptive narrative: people are learning to distrust the culture industry, things may be getting better. However, a close reading of Adorno's earlier essays would soon show that not only is his account never wholly negative (however close it may get) – in fact in numerous comments Adorno attests to what survives or resists the culture industry: 'Traces of something better persist in those features of the culture industry by which it resembles the circus – in the stubbornly purposeless expertise of riders, acrobats and clowns' (DE 114) – but he explicitly registers the resistance which the culture industry generates to its own activities. People learn to recognize and see through what the industry claims they need, which is why the culture industry needs to continually evolve in order to produce or satisfy new needs. This is after all, the only consistent position which Adorno can take up, if only to account for the possibility of his own work. If the triumph and dominance of the culture industry really were total, how would any criticism be possible at all?

If Adorno were to simply issue instructions for resistance or approval of particular art works, he would be simply assimilated to the culture industry, and the chance of contributing to some kind of progress would evaporate. His work needs to provoke the same kind of attention and concentration that a Schoenberg piece does. As with criticism of art, so with our reading of Adorno we must insist that 'not knowing what one sees or hears bestows no privileged direct relation to works but instead makes their perception impossible' (AT 338). In other words before we rush to judgement we need to ensure we know what we're looking at. In the case of the cartoons Adorno and Horkheimer seem to have condemned out of hand, a little background research can tell us that they are in fact commenting on the major transformation of the form of the animated seven-minute cartoon short after 1937, in which the chase came to dominate. So much so in fact that this violent, relentless, hugely entertaining and apparently completely amoral genre has come to epitomize the form, as Matt Groening's cartoon-within-cartoon homage to the classic cat and mouse pairing in *The Simpsons, Itchy and Scratchy*, demonstrates. A reaction against the staid and moralizing melodramas of the thirties (dismissed by veteran animators as 'birds and bees pictures' or 'boy scout pictures'[10]), and pioneered by Warner Bros., chase cartoons were also significantly cheaper to make, and so more attractive for the studios. With America's entry into the Second World War, they also proved ideally suited for Nazi-bashing propaganda. Once we bear all this in mind, it becomes easier to hear not the disapproval, but the sympathy for an art form which has once offered a kind of 'justice' for the 'mutilated' cast-offs of western capitalist culture.

AESTHETIC THEORY AND IDEOLOGY-CRITIQUE

In 1979 the French sociologist Pierre Bourdieu published a work entitled *Distinction: A Social Critique of the Judgement of Taste*. Although Bourdieu is hardly a household name in the English-speaking world, his work is increasingly influential within the academy, while in France his prestige has ensured that his work has been related to educational and cultural questions in forming legislation. The reason Bourdieu is interesting here is that his work typifies a common contemporary reaction to the idea of the aesthetic, a reaction which passes for 'common sense' in many places, but which is turned into a methodological and political principle in others. His position is hardly new, indeed Adorno responds to a similar argument in his essay on Thorstein Veblen in *Prisms*, but it suggests something of the fate of the aesthetic tradition in contemporary society, and thus the lasting worth of Adorno's interrogation of that tradition.

Bourdieu argues that what we call 'taste' is in fact a highly complex marker of social position. In other words, he denies the claim of the adherents of the aesthetic tradition that the perception of the aesthetic is a universal human faculty. He suggests instead that this tradition confuses aesthetic with economic value, and that the appreciation of culture is as much a valuable asset as individual paintings, which may command great prices at auction. For Bourdieu, even an education system which claims to educate all children equally fails in the face of class differences in the relationship to culture: a child whose parents take her to museums and play classical music will be distinguished from a child whose parents do not. If the appreciation of the aesthetic is not in fact universal, but learnt, then the claims made on behalf of the importance of art are merely a mask for social domination. Bourdieu uses the idea of culture as a whole to threaten the privilege attached to the more restricted notion of culture: 'one cannot fully understand cultural practices unless "culture", in the restricted, normative sense of ordinary usage, is brought back into "culture" in the anthropological sense'.[11] If 'high culture' is only another form of culture in general, the privilege the aesthetic tradition attaches to art which satisfies disinterested contemplation rather than more immediate gratifications (and implies formal or abstract art rather than mimetic, descriptive or narrative forms), has no normative claim.

Positioning Adorno in relation to an argument like Bourdieu's is complex. As in the case of the distinction between modernism and the avant-garde, Adorno can be seen on both sides at once. Now Adorno would certainly agree with Bourdieu that from the very inception, if not before, of the Romantic notion of the aesthetic, art has been a social marker. Indeed the greater the extent to which art has claimed to withdraw from society, from utility and from commercial exchange, the more such value it acquires. So Adorno is in no sense a naïve defender of the aesthetic tradition. In 'Theory of Pseudo-Culture' he argues that 'the qualities which the word "culture" acquired [following the rise of the bourgeoisie to political power] allowed the rising class to achieve its goals in economy and administration'. In fact, he goes further than Bourdieu in identifying culture not just with art, but with a whole way of life: 'without culture the bourgeois would hardly have succeeded as entrepreneur, middleman, civil servant or anything at all' (TPC 20–1). Even more like Bourdieu, Adorno suggests that 'by denying it can be bought, culture becomes entangled in the network of privilege – only those who have it need not buy and possess it' (TPC 26). But at the same time, Adorno insists that the possibilities released by the development of the idea of culture are not wholly contaminated by their origins. Art's promise to abolish class distinctions and to release society as a whole (not just the individual viewer of or listener to an artwork) remains alive, in however attenuated a form. At the apex of Kant's critical philosophy, the possibility of aesthetic judgement as a faculty common to all men secures the ground of an existence which moves beyond the mere satisfaction of primary needs such as food and shelter. This is also the premise for art's universality. For Adorno the fact that art turns out to have a commercial value is no accident, but an essential corollary of its possible autonomy, which in a world based on exchange is almost immediately turned back into a commodity.

Bourdieu presumes he can find a rational ground from which to condemn aesthetics, considered here as an ideology. In other words, Bourdieu believes he can tell the difference between true and false, and that the normative claim of the aesthetic is false. From Adorno's point of view this is not only naïve, but involves an element of bad faith. If Adorno were to claim to have an objective and neutral standpoint from which he can simply see that the culture industry has distorted people's needs, that the culture industry supplies cultural goods people do not want or need alongside or instead of those they do, he would also have to be able to explain why he was able to see this, while others could not. To criticize ideology seems to require a philosophical ground. This is the situation into which Marxist criticism falls very rapidly, and requires the invention of the idea of ideology: ideology being that false consciousness which needs to be replaced by the truth which Marxist science claims to supply. The reason why everyone else should be wrong, and the Marxist correct, is never adequately explained. Adorno recognizes the bankruptcy of this argument, and responds in two ways.

Firstly, he dismisses the notion that people are somehow duped by the culture industry. Adorno's position would be untenable if resistance was solely the preserve of the cultural critic: we would have fallen back into the myth of the intellectual as prophet or seer. His stress on the elimination of both popular and autonomous art by the culture industry means that neither from above nor below can we identify some kind of authentic or natural space in which music is not consumed in terms of its exchange value rather than its use value. But resistance is provoked by the mechanisms of distribution and production themselves. The continual consumption of musical goods depends on the repetition of the ever-same, that is the exchangeable rather than the 'new' (which is the hallmark of successful art). But the public would not accept the repetition of the same songs over and over, so the industry needs to produce new songs, and there will always be a tension between the variation of cultural products and their underlying sameness. The more the songs are the same, the less able they are to interest people, the more they produce a resistance to the industrial production of culture as a whole; but equally, familiarity breeds contempt. This inexorable movement in the industry is determined by the resistance which the industry provokes to itself. Note that this is not a resistance onto which we could fasten as a stimulus for political change: it is more like a negative testimony to the success of bourgeois cultural production in obliterating the possibility of popular art, and autonomous art. Resistance is going on: 'What appears to be ready acceptance and unproblematic gratification,' Adorno argues, 'is actually of a very complex nature . . . Mass listening habits today are *ambivalent*' (EOM 463). But such resistance cannot be thematized, made the basis for criticism or a political intervention, because such a movement can itself only pass through culture, and through the contaminated forms of rational thought, or aesthetic distance. Because for the critic to affirm their own autonomy would be to invent an illusory separation between their position and that of the brainwashed masses, the critic can only affirm negatively the incompleteness of the domination of the exchange principle.

Secondly, Adorno stresses that cultural criticism is itself part of the culture industry, and that as a result the idea of ideology is problematic. In his programmatic essay 'Cultural Criticism and Society' he argues that 'there are no more ideologies in the authentic sense of false consciousness, only advertisements for the world through its duplication and the provocative lie which does not seek belief but commands silence' (P 34). He also turns over this problem in one of the fragments of *Minima Moralia*. He questions the assumption that culture can be reduced to 'ideology', seen as the illusory veil thrown over the real material functioning of society. We might see this as the most distinctive modern form of the Platonic allegory of the cave, in which the philosopher can see the true forms, of which most people can only see the shadows cast on the wall of the cave. Even critics of philosophy as the science of the true as different as Marx and Nietzsche risk reinventing an inverted philosophy in which the everyday practices of life are stripped away to reveal the mechanisms underneath. Adorno suggests that less subtle followers of both men have done just that. Here Adorno's sense of dialectics intervenes: the idea of ideology as a lie tends to turn rapidly into a lie itself. Claiming to reveal the 'truth' behind the lies is a case of throwing out the baby with the bathwater. So while Adorno agrees that much of what passes for everyday existence may seem like a cloak thrown over the exploitation and violence of capitalism and needs to be exposed,

> to act radically in accordance with this principle would be to extirpate with the false, all that was true also, all that, however impotent, strives to escape the confines of universal practice, every chimerical anticipation of a nobler condition, and so to bring about directly the barbarism that culture is reproached with furthering indirectly. (MM 44)

Like Nietzsche, Adorno here seems to consider the distinction between truth and lies misleading: where Nietzsche distinguishes a creative lie from a lie that has grown old and has been forgotten as a lie, Adorno sees a need for some lies in order to combat other lies. Culture may not be possible as an alternative, but it may be the best possible way to criticize the state of things. However, because of his acute awareness of the dialectics of culture, of its tendency to capitulate to society and form a kind of compensatory reserve, the critic's relationship with culture will always be ambiguous. A theory of ideology will either be partial, in leaving the position of the critic unaccounted for, or irrational, since when everything becomes ideology there would be nothing left against which to judge its falsehood. The hypothesis of a truth of experience beyond theoretical reflection serves as a provisional anchor for Adorno's critique.

Adorno recognizes that the question of art cannot simply be detached from that of the other standards by which we judge and assess the world. His recognition that there can be no simple opposition or alternative position, no 'outside' of the social world keeps him from taking up Bourdieu's position. There has always been, and will always be, an element of bad faith in claiming to take a vantage point outside the social processes and to criticize from there, not least because the necessary correlative is a sense of ideology as the false consciousness of everyone except you. The critic, like the artist, will always be caught up in the same social processes which he or she seeks to criticize. So the critic is faced with only the materials of society with which to effect its critique. This places the critic in an awkward position: how to continue to insist that the world might be something other than it is, without assuming any conception of another type of society, which may always turn out to be a fantastic projection of some aspect of that society, or to secretly function to sustain that society. What Adorno's friend Herbert Marcuse diagnosed as the problem of affirmative culture, in which even the apparently critical elements of society play a role in maintaining the functioning of the whole, is writ large as the entire problem of thinking, and of living, in an unjust society. Cultural criticism must take place from within culture. It must depend on the very concepts it wants to question, or is unsure about. Whereas the critique of ideology can (and often does) pretend to an objective or scientific standpoint, to better enforce its own position, cultural criticism can admit that its procedure must be circular and reflexive, and in one sense experimental, in trying to suspect those premises and complicities which make it possible, but which block change.

The final sections of Adorno's essay 'Theory of Pseudo-Culture' provide a clear example of these themes, and will allow us a preliminary characterization of his critical approach. In the face of the administered world of the culture industry 'the only way spirit can survive is through critical reflection on pseudo-culture, for which culture is essential' (TPC 38). Such critical reflection would in effect confirm the survival of culture within its deformed surrogate. Unlike Bourdieu, for whom the idea of aesthetics and culture is to be called into question from the outside as ideology, Adorno insists that 'the illusion that anyone – and by this one always means oneself – might be exempt from the tendency to socialized pseudo-culture' is 'conceited' (TPC 37). Because the possibility of culture is directly linked to its historical situation, this reflection on culture must take place from inside, or as Adorno sees it in *Negative Dialectics*: 'Dialectics is the self-consciousness of the objective context of delusion; it does not mean to have escaped from that concept. Its objective goal is to break out of that context from within' (ND 406). The critique of ideology depends on a prior escape: dialectics cannot assume that such an escape is possible. Rather than evading Bourdieu's critique of culture, Adorno extends it to the point where even critical reflection must be understood as participating in the dialectic of culture and barbarism: 'an alloy of barbarism is mixed like an enzyme with progress itself, with the category of the new'. For this reason, the objective of criticism is not the purification of culture through the removal of pseudo-culture but the transcendence of the 'antithesis of culture (*Bildung*) and the lack of it, of culture (*Kultur*) and nature' (TPC 37). All that can be achieved through the ideologist's attack on culture is its destruction.

Lest Adorno's conception of the task of cultural criticism should seem equally negative, we should remember that there is a positive principle intermingled with it. The analysis of aesthetic and cultural artefacts in terms of their historical components denies them their autonomy. But only if we hold to an organic account of the unity of the aesthetic object is this an end rather than a beginning. In fact Adorno could be seen to affirm the starting point of a new mode of cultural analysis, which through showing the impurity of aesthetics, that the art work is shot through with historical and social material, not only destroys the idea of culture as something higher, but is also able to acknowledge art's essential involvement with what it seeks to cast out as its opposite.

CHAPTER 3

FREEDOM AND SOCIETY

There is no moral certainty. Its mere assumption would be immoral, would falsely relieve the individual of anything that might be called morality.

(ND 242–3)

A free man would only be one who need not bow to any alternatives, and under existing circumstances there is a touch of freedom in refusing to accept the alternatives. Freedom means to criticise and change situations, not to confirm them by deciding within their coercive structures.

(ND 226)

There is a photograph of Adorno taken in Los Angeles in the 1940s. In the portrait Adorno is seated facing away from the camera, but screwed around in his chair, looking backwards over his shoulder at the photographer, as if, although the photograph seems obviously posed, the philosopher had been surprised at his desk. Adorno's sturdy wooden writing cabinet, the desktop of which has been folded down to reveal a number of drawers, towers over him. On the precipitous top of the cabinet are a number of toy giraffes, while a little further down, a small monkey sits on a ledge. One of the giraffes seems to be peering over, as if keeping a benevolent eye on Teddy, a man who took as his own familiar name that of a soft toy. Underneath his large rounded spectacles, Adorno has a half-smile: the effect is decidedly goofy, hardly the portrait one might imagine of the severe and critical intellectual exile.

Discussing this photograph, Robert Savage reminds us of Adorno's propensity for using animal-related nicknames. Adorno and his wife Gretel were cow and hippopotamus; indeed Adorno would on occasion refer to himself as 'Archibald the Hippo King'.[1] Adorno's biographer Lorenz Jäger also remarks on his regular use of animal imagery. For example, writing to Horkheimer in 1941 about their imminent move to LA, Adorno remarks that 'it is better if the horses are transported by rail'.[2] For Jäger, Adorno's love of animals is faintly ridiculous, and at one with his love of nature, a romantic inclination which underpins the story the biographer wants to tell about his subject's withdrawal from the messy and mundane world of politics. Yet the idea of nature for Adorno is absolutely not that of a prelapsarian idyll, an antidote to the noxious atmosphere of modern society. The conclusion to a lengthy fragment titled 'Man and Beast', appended to *Dialectic of Enlightenment*, gives us some idea of the complexity of nature for both Adorno and Horkheimer:

> Nature itself is neither good, as was believed by the old Romanticism, nor noble, as is asserted by the new. As a model and a goal it signifies anti-intellectualism, lies, bestiality; only when apprehended as knowledge does it become the urge of the living toward peace, the consciousness which, from the beginning, has inspired the unerring resistance to *Führer* and collective. What threatens the prevailing praxis and its inescapable alternatives is not nature, with which that praxis coincides, but the remembrance of nature. (DE 211–12)

This is a rewriting of Adorno's understanding of the task of philosophy as the critical investigation of second nature, not in order to provide access to a living, more vital or authentic reality, but to trace the absence, the outline of what is missing, the way modern life fails to live up to the promises made for it.

So the fact that Adorno refers to animals when he is at his silliest only serves to counterpoint the importance of the idea of nature throughout his work. Adorno often has recourse to animals at crucial points in his account of moral philosophy. In *Minima Moralia*, for example, he argues that:

> The possibility of pogroms is decided in the moment when the gaze of a fatally wounded animal falls on a human being. The defiance with which he repels this gaze – 'after all it's only an animal' – reappears irresistibly in cruelties done to human beings, the perpetrators having again and again to reassure themselves that it is 'only

an animal,' because they could never fully believe this even of animals. (MM 105)

Or to paraphrase Adorno's typically cryptic formulation, man's attempt to set himself apart from animals never quite convinces anyone. Man remains an animal, and secretly knows this, so the distinction which serves to legitimate his inhumanity to other creatures will always fail as a justification. There is a direct connection between man's cruelty to animals and the worst atrocities committed on other human beings: in other words, anti-Semitism becomes not an irrational aberration in an otherwise orderly and rational world, but intimately associated with the idea of reason itself. The possibility of free, rational, moral action which forms the cornerstone of moral philosophy in the Kantian tradition is founded on a capacity which, in dividing man from the animals, allows both man's indifference to the suffering of animals, and his forgetting of their kinship.

This is an argument that can be directly recast in cultural terms. As Adorno and Horkheimer argue in *Dialectic of Enlightenment*, man's attempt to set himself apart from nature is bound up with the domination of nature, which reveals that man has not in fact escaped nature after all: 'Civilization is the triumph of society over nature – a triumph which transforms everything into mere nature' (DE 153). If culture, society, those institutions which protect us from the power of the natural world over man, really only perpetuate the violent passions of man's own animal nature, we learn two things: that all these concepts are less decisive and more ambiguous than they might seem at first; and that the Kantian tradition of moral thought, in which the possibility of right living is directly linked to the free use of one's reason, can no longer be considered adequate. These two impulses lie at the bottom of Adorno's writing on morality, freedom and society. On the one hand, as in his work on aesthetics, he seems to uphold basic Kantian assumptions about the value of a free autonomous moral judgement. On the other, parallel to the critical side of his aesthetic theory, Adorno suggests that not only may society prohibit such a free use of one's reason (a Hegelian argument), but that the problematic interweaving of the concepts of reason and morality may itself render the idea of living a good life an impossibility (a line which owes more to Nietzsche).

Because they revolve around this apparent impossibility of living rightly, Adorno's moral writings can appear almost hysterical. Like his writing on popular culture – to which these moral questions are directly linked – Adorno seems concerned only to indict ordinary existence on moral grounds. This chapter will explore this apparent severity, looking first at Adorno's insistence on the moral inadequacy of even a simple trip to the cinema. Such severity can be best understood if Adorno is seen as playing the role of Kant, who figures as the pre-eminent moral philosopher of the modern era; and the second section of the chapter will establish how Adorno responds to Kant. The third section of the chapter will examine the way Adorno juxtaposes the moral demands of Kant with the reality of a society in which such behaviour does not seem possible, while the fourth section explores Adorno's seductive but problematic attempt to give a genealogical account of this situation in *Dialectic of Enlightenment*, possibly his most famous book, co-written with Horkheimer. The chapter closes with two sets of conclusions to be drawn from the preceding discussion: the first is of immense importance in understanding Adorno's work as a whole, and links his revised idea of materialism to his understanding of the nature of the concept; the second returns directly to the question of wrong living, and asks what the value of Adorno's discussion of morality might be for our own everyday life.

Much of Adorno's moral thinking can be extrapolated from *Dialectic of Enlightenment*, but *Minima Moralia* is the more successful work: what is given a genealogical and apparently straightforwardly historical description in the former is presented in aporetic terms in the latter – aporetic meaning that Adorno presents us with conflicting moral demands, neither of which can be assumed to overrule the other. The danger is that we may be misled by the narrative of the former work, which claims to account for the irresolvable dilemmas diagnosed by the latter, to see the resolution of moral difficulties as itself historical. Other major sources for our understanding of Adorno's moral thinking are some sections of *Negative Dialectics*, particularly the intricate reading of Kant on freedom, and the final sections on the possibility of metaphysics after Auschwitz. The material for these sections is also covered in two of Adorno's published lecture courses, *The Problems of Moral Philosophy* and the final meetings of his course on *Metaphysics: Concepts and Problems*. We should, however, be slightly wary of relying too heavily on these. Adorno's lectures, although based on his notes for whatever major work was in progress at the time, naturally take a very different form to the more complete (and often more cryptic, or dialectical) formulation of the same ideas in his published work. In consequence, they should not be taken as definitive statements of a thought which centres on the difficulty of giving definite answers, and focuses on the questions of both metaphysics and morals, as the titles of the courses suggest, as things that must remain problematic.

WRONG LIFE: ADORNO'S *MINIMA MORALIA*

A garish screenprint by Eduardo Paolozzi is entitled 'Wittgenstein at the Cinema admires Betty Grable'. Brightly coloured stripes are juxtaposed with the silhouettes of two cartoon mice with familiar Walt Disney ears, set against a background grid of small black and white diamonds. A cut-away diagram of a Messerschmitt fighter aircraft hangs menacingly in the top right-hand corner. Below the image is printed a description of the Austrian philosopher's habit of proceeding to the cinema directly after he had finished a lecture: 'He insisted on sitting in the very first row of seats, so that the screen would occupy his entire field of vision . . . He wished to become totally absorbed in the film no matter how trivial or artificial it was, in order to free his mind temporarily from the philosophical thoughts that tortured and exhausted him.'[3] Wittgenstein is hardly the only philosopher to have visited the cinema. Indeed thinkers as diverse as Gilles Deleuze and Stanley Cavell have taken cinema seriously as more than a mere distraction from philosophy, even as the pre-eminent art form of the twentieth century. So it may come as some surprise to find Adorno so uncompromising on the subject: 'Every visit to the cinema', Adorno writes, 'leaves me, against all my vigilance, stupider and worse' (MM 25).

The extreme dialectical style of *Minima Moralia*, which counterposes hyperbolic and conflicting propositions in an attempt to keep thought moving, might allow us to place such an apparently over-the-top claim in brackets, as a moment in Adorno's thought, no more. But returning to the topic more than ten years later in his lecture course on the *Problems of Moral Philosophy* (1962/3) Adorno seems equally certain, and equally severe:

I would almost go so far as to say that even the apparently harmless visit to the cinema to which we condemn ourselves should really be accompanied by the realization that such visits are actually a betrayal of the insights we have acquired and that they will probably entangle us – admittedly only to an infinitesimal degree, but assuredly with a cumulative effect – in the processes that will transform us into what we are supposed to become and what we are making of ourselves in order to enable us to survive, and to ensure that we conform. (PMP 168)

This is in part a lesson in Adorno's revised conception of the dialectic: its moments are not, as they are in Hegel, to be overcome or surpassed in some higher synthesis. The categorical imperative not to go to the cinema cannot simply be dismissed or dissolved, once we have grasped its function in Adorno's argument. Accounting for what seems to be such ludicrous overbidding in his work is one of the most perplexing aspects of reading and responding to Adorno. By asking why he is so insistent on this topic we can resolve some of the more cryptic pronouncements in *Minima Moralia* which present a constellation of ideas to which he will return again and again: both Adorno's method and his social thought are fully formed by the time *Minima Moralia*, dated 1944–47, is published in 1951.

One of the great strengths of Adorno's writing is his ability to connect the largest metaphysical questions to the smallest details of human existence. As he argues in the introduction to *Minima Moralia*, this is in part an inheritance from Hegel. As we saw in the introduction to this book, Adorno values Hegel and Beethoven for the tension their works maintain between the individual and the total, between the part and the whole, but he is suspicious that in both cases the small becomes a mere moment in the greater whole. Adorno's work seeks to maintain that tension, as the form of *Minima Moralia* suggests. The book is arranged in three sequences of fragments, each of which ranges over topics from family life through to world history, from a child's experience of the zoo to Adorno's criticisms of Hegel. Nothing, it seems, should be exempt from the gaze of the moral philosopher, but the connections are not filled in. The fragments hang together in the form of the book, but do not add up to an all-encompassing theory. But in wiring even the most apparently innocent details of everyday life directly to moral absolutes, Adorno seems to put into action a paranoid inversion of the totalitarian tendencies he discerns within contemporary society, as if even the smallest moment of joy should be constantly overshadowed by the threat of disaster. In his lectures on metaphysics, he inverts

Hannah Arendt's comments on the banality of evil. Evil may be banal, but for Adorno the banal becomes suspect in its turn: 'triviality is evil – triviality, that is, as the form of consciousness and mind that adapts itself to the world as it is, that obeys the principle of inertia. And this principle of inertia truly is what is radically evil' (MCP 115). But this is only a restatement of the comment with which he prefaces his complaint about the cinema, that 'there is nothing innocuous left' (MM 25).

Adorno's resistance to the idea of the harmless visit to the cinema may seem all the more surprising when we bear in mind that two of his closest friends before the war had been intensely interested in the analysis of film. Both Siegfried Kracauer and Walter Benjamin, in dialogue with whom many of Adorno's earliest ideas were forged, published major works on the significance of cinema. But where Kracauer saw the new mass cultural forms as heralding the demise of bourgeois notions of subjectivity, and Benjamin saw the technical innovations of film as opening the way for a new revolutionary proletariat which might defeat fascism, Adorno sees only a threat to the autonomy of the individual. Kracauer characterized the cinema in one essay in terms of the 'cult of distraction': the superficial splendour of the new Berlin picture palaces, the spotlights and music inside, all serve to expose 'the disorder of society' and 'evoke and maintain that tension which must precede the inevitable and radical change'.[4] For Benjamin, film was one of the new technological art processes whose estrangement of the world could provoke radical change, both aesthetic and political. Adorno levelled similar objections to both: Benjamin he accused of 'an anarchistic romanticism of blind confidence in the spontaneous power of the proletariat in the historical process' which he links directly to one of Kracauer's favourite directors: 'the idea that a reactionary is turned into a member of the avant-garde by expert knowledge of Chaplin's films strikes me as out-and-out romanticization'.[5] This cannot be a matter of different tastes, as Adorno himself admired Chaplin, and was delighted to be imitated by him at a Hollywood party in the 1940s. Nor can we put it down to pessimism rather than optimism. Adorno's reservations are derived from theoretical concerns with his friend's approach. This dispute, couched in moral terms in *Minima Moralia*, is also both political and philosophical. This should remind us that these categories can rarely be disentangled in Adorno's writing.

What Benjamin, Kracauer and Adorno shared in the 1920s, but which Adorno comes to question, is an attempt to decipher or interpret the smallest details of everyday life as fragments of the whole social world, with an eye to the redemption of the whole. In reaction to the systematic metaphysics of Idealist philosophy, but equally suspicious of the dominant neo-Kantian epistemology which by dividing historical from philosophical enquiry appeared to renounce the possibility of grasping the ultimate unity of philosophy and history, they turned to a radical nominalism. An unflinching attention to the apparently insignificant or overlooked artefacts and forms of life was to be the antidote to philosophy's inherent tendency to subsume the particular under the concept, and to obliterate the messiness of the real world with the abstraction of logic. Such careful attention to the discarded and to the forgotten was to redeem the whole, in a more or less overtly theological paradigm which synthesized elements of avant-garde art and Jewish messianism. As the political situation in Weimar Germany deteriorated, this subterranean theology was more or less covertly transfigured into an avowedly Marxist framework. In fact the separation of cultural critique from questions of political mobilization and party organization, for which Adorno is generally attacked, is already complete in Benjamin's late works, for example. The difference between the friends arose from Adorno's refusal to accept the social revision of the theological premises which had always worried him. Equally concerned with the overturning of the social order, he refused to accept that it was either realistic or desirable to look for such an upheaval from the vast majority of the population. The task of the intellectual should not be to find premonitions of revolution in the wreckage of the old order, but to launch an attack on both the old order *and* those movements which claimed to be able to transform it. The intellectual consistency of Adorno's position is based on the disavowal of any claim to a privileged point of view for the intellectual as an observer of society. Why should a way out be apparent to one individual but not to the vast mass of the population? The fragment following his comments on cinema warns us that 'he who stands aloof runs the risk of believing himself better than others and misusing his critique of society as an ideology for his own private interest' (MM 26). The inherent elitism of avant-garde art, politics and theory was anathema to Adorno, and this lays the ground for the divergence between his own work and the common or garden varieties of Marxist ideology critique.

Minima Moralia is Adorno's response. The method he had shared with his friends is now more explicitly grounded not in the detached observation of objective fragments of the social totality, but in the individual's subjective experience of it and reflection on it. This enables Adorno to reformulate the vague political and social aspirations of his friends in explicitly moral terms. So it is significant that what he objects to in the cinema is not cast here in terms of its effects on its audience as a whole – in contrast to his remarks in his letter to Benjamin, where he describes the 'laughter of the audience at the cinema' as being 'full of the worst kind of bourgeois sadism'. Adorno has, he says, 'discussed this with Max [Horkheimer]', and in *Dialectic of Enlightenment* the two suggest that cinemas are good only because they allow the unemployed to find 'freshness in summer and warmth in winter' in what is otherwise a 'bloated entertainment apparatus [which] does not make life more worthy of human beings' (DE 111).[6] Here the question is posed in terms not of the social whole, but of individual morality: how can you (or I) justify spending time in the cinema? That this is indeed Adorno's intention can be confirmed by reference to other parts of *Minima Moralia*. If cinema will make us stupid, this can be helpfully linked to his claim that 'Intelligence is a moral category' (MM 197) and the understanding, derived ultimately from Kant, that at the centre of morality lies 'autonomy and responsibility' (MM 198). If I am at the cinema, I am resigning myself to the world as it is, going along with the flow, rather than seeking to raise myself above it. I am giving up rather than fighting against the way things are, surrendering to the pressure of existence to conform: 'all collaboration, all the human worth of social mixing and participation, merely masks a tacit acceptance of inhumanity', Adorno adds, a few lines after his remarks on the cinema (MM 26).

Adorno sees *Minima Moralia* as a reminder of a role 'which from time immemorial was regarded as the true field of philosophy, but which, since the latter's conversion into method, has lapsed into intellectual neglect, sententious whimsy and finally oblivion: the teaching of the good life' (MM 15). This does not mean that Adorno believes that philosophy (or *Minima Moralia* itself) can any longer teach us how to live a good life. Objective social conditions prevent it: on this Adorno is absolutely insistent. If the task of the philosopher ought to be to show us how to live, this is no longer possible: 'Wrong life cannot be lived rightly' (MM 39). That this is the keynote of Adorno's moral thought is confirmed in his later lectures on moral philosophy, which regularly refer back to *Minima Moralia* as 'a book on the good – or rather the bad – life' (PMP 1), Adorno maintains this view: 'in the bad life, the good life cannot be lived' (PMP 167).

In later years Adorno formulated these questions over and over again, seeking to understand the possibility of living a moral life in a world in which such disasters as the Holocaust are possible. In his lecture of 20 July 1965, Adorno described this in terms of 'the guilt in which one is enmeshed almost by the mere fact of continuing to live' which 'can hardly be reconciled any longer with life itself'. My existence turns out to be indefensible in moral terms. How can I justify my life: 'by continuing to live one is taking away that possibility from someone else, to whom life has been denied; that one is stealing a person's life' (MCP 112–3). This takes its fullest form in the aphorism that in wrong life, one cannot live, repeated in *Minima Moralia* and the lectures on moral philosophy. Or as Adorno puts it in his lectures:

> If we – each of us sitting here – knew at every moment what has happened and to what concatenations we owe our own existence, and how our own existence is interwoven with calamity, even if we have done nothing wrong, simply by having neglected, through fear, to help other people at a crucial moment, for example – a situation very familiar to me from the time of the Third Reich – if one were fully aware of all these things at every moment, one would really be unable to live. One is pushed as it were, into forgetfulness, which is already a form of guilt. By failing to be aware at every moment of what threatens and what has happened, one also contributes to it; one resists it too little; and it can be repeated and reinstated at any moment. (MCP 113)

Although Adorno's comments explicitly refer to the events of the Nazi period in German history, and also raise the immense political question of the extent to which the post-war reconstruction of Germany should involve remembrance rather than forgetting of what had happened, we would be wrong to assume that his remarks only apply in such a situation. In *Minima Moralia* the context is clearly broader: and in fact it is the concept of duty or of right living itself which is at stake here. Adorno tries to think moral philosophy to its limit, to the point at which it is overwhelmed by the factual, material process of destruction in which it is enmeshed. Capitalism is a world-wide system of exploitation. My wealth or leisure is bought at the price of someone else's labour. My freedom of action is bought at the price of someone else's. From a standpoint which refuses the idea of fate or election of the individual, my survival can only be a matter of chance, of luck. There is nothing to justify this. When Adorno asks what it might mean to live after Auschwitz, he is really asking about the possibility of a moral philosophy once we have removed its metaphysical or supernatural elements, and once we confront it with the facts of the world with which it claims to propose a way of reconciling my existence.

ADORNO AND KANT

The question of a visit to the cinema turns out to be a question of morality. To see Adorno's grounds for posing this challenge, but also how such a challenge fits into his thought as a whole, we need an account of his understanding of moral philosophy. At the centre of Adorno's moral philosophy lies the work of Immanuel Kant. It is not that Adorno agrees with Kant, or that Kant's moral theory is correct: since a philosophy is always of its time, there could be no question of simply transplanting moral reasoning from one age to another. Rather what Kant represents for Adorno is the most rigorous and coherent account of morality. It is, he comments in his lectures of 1962/3, 'moral philosophy *par excellence*, moral philosophy as such'. Kant provides us with 'a fully articulated and logically consistent philosophy of morality' (PMP 106). This does not imply that Adorno endorses Kantian morality: the question he is interested in is precisely the possibility of upholding such a moral theory today. But we need to understand the idea of morality before we can judge it. Moreover, Adorno is also recommending the best way to think about morality, even if it is no longer wholly adequate. Remember that any philosophy is inextricably bound to its social context, and Adorno's sense of the 'truth' of the thinkers he discusses comes not from their logical validity, but from the relationship between the thought and its world.

What is important about Kant for Adorno is the rigour with which he isolates and examines the concept of morality. This concept is based around the notion of freedom, or in more Kantian terms, autonomy. Autonomy means dictating the law (*nomos*) by which I act for myself (*autos*), rather than following a rule that has come from outside, acting heteronomously. Or put more plainly, for Kant a moral decision is one that I make of my own free choice. A decision which I make that has been based on merely conforming to what is expected of me according to the customs of a particular community is not free. Thus we cannot learn anything about what we ought or ought not to do from studying the actions of those around us and copying what seem to be the prevailing ways of behaviour. A theory of morals cannot be derived from the observation of merely empirical moral behaviour, of what people generally call good and bad. This has practical and theoretical consequences. Although for Kant morality is linked in principle to a rejection of social customs, as of religious authority, in practice it will turn out his views are pretty much in line with the values of his day. Equally, we do not act morally, or freely, if we are only acting out of anything other than rational reflection. Acting in accordance with our passions, our desires, or even out of physical necessity, cannot be moral. In this sense, there is a deeply critical element to Kant's moral thought, which means setting oneself against society, tradition, or political authority, in order to act upon your own will. This is also an overcoming of our own nature by reason, once we accept that the various emotional and physical impulses which we feel are compulsions to act.

However, this does not mean that my actions are free simply if they are autonomous rather than heteronomous: decided upon by my will, rather than dictated by some external or internal drive or pressure. Kant restores a normative sense of morality by arguing that my actions are only moral if they match up to the moral law: paradoxically, freedom comes through acting in accordance with a law. This law is universal, in that it is the maxim that one should act as one would wish others to act. In its contact with the universal in the concrete moral judgement, reason and necessity are linked. Reason and freedom lie in the overcoming of nature, autonomy must come from the overcoming of heteronomy. Without the idea of the universal, there can be no morality. For Adorno, Kant's account establishes an essential link between reason, freedom and the universal, without which there can be no morality. After Kant, moral thinking can no longer be derived from custom – based on the way things have always been done, or the way the people around us do things – while at the same time avoiding the relativism of treating everybody's way of doing things as equally worthy of respect. Without this link, there can be no normative account of morality.

Only a decision which has not been dictated by necessity, or by my desires, can count as moral: morality is more than mere survival. The complication is that this starts to look rather like its opposite, a confusion Adorno explores in his lectures: to act in accordance with the moral law looks formally similar to acting in conformity with the customs or laws of a particular community, to doing nothing more than what is expected of me. But for Kant, even if what I do is in accord with the moral law, to do it out of self-interest, rather than out of respect for the law itself, cannot be described as moral. Adorno will follow Kant's account of moral autonomy, as the most rigorous and impressive account of morality; and he underlines the extent to which this account, carried through to its end, means a struggle not only against social conformism, but against the impulses and instincts of the self, against human nature. Adorno underlines in his lectures 'the massive and almost inhuman harshness and severity with which Kant excludes from his moral philosophy everything to do with happiness', and 'the suppression of, above all, every natural impulse, the suppression of affection and the suppression of sympathy' (PMP 71). Morality for Adorno is a process of overcoming: an overcoming of self; an overcoming of nature; and an overcoming of society.

It is closely linked with the idea of a critical philosophy, a philosophy which comes to criticize not only the world, but itself, for it cannot deny that philosophy is also part of the world. The Kantian critical and moral impulse lies at the core of Adorno's project. His revision of Hegel often seems to be carried out with an eye on Kant. Where Hegel constructs a speculative philosophy of the end of history from which we can see how antinomies are resolved, Kant starts where we are, in the middle of a difficult and irreconciled world. He is concerned to establish the possible grounds on which an adequate criticism of the world might be possible, considering how thought might be said to make contact with reality – with the concrete objective details which are subsumed into the totality of the historical process in Hegel, against which Adorno protests. But it should be clear from the preceding discussion that the problem of man's domination over nature can be directly detected in this Kantian conception of morality, but also therefore in the idea of a critical philosophy which guides Adorno's own work. Freedom for Kant means freedom from nature: an overcoming not only of any external compulsion to act in a certain way, but also of our own desires, and of what we tend to think of as natural instincts such as pity, compassion, sympathy. Heteronomy comes from within as well as without: moral autonomy means a victory over any human nature as much as the pressures of society or the natural world. Overcoming morality means emancipation from both good and evil: for Adorno such an overcoming entails an equal suspicion of any 'natural' moral sentiments, as of the socially accepted way of doing things. But it then comes to mean a suspicion of morality, and of reason, itself.

As in his cultural criticism, the solution for Adorno is to attempt to conceive of the world from two points of view at once, as if from within and without. In *Minima Moralia* Adorno speaks in places from behind the mask of the moral philosopher: this is I think the case with the ban on the trip to the cinema. This does not simply imply that Adorno does not mean what he says: on the contrary he is deadly serious, since the very possibility of morality, of reason, and of freedom depends on it. This problem of freedom emerges only obliquely in *Minima Moralia*, yet it is everywhere presupposed by it. So where Wittgenstein can use the cinema as an escape from the pressure of his philosophical torments, for Adorno that escape route is specifically marked as evasion or capitulation. The argument that this is only a harmless diversion, mere entertainment, is ruled out in advance by the understanding of freedom as autonomy which Adorno inherits from Kant. If I freely choose to attend the cinema, perhaps I am at least not neglecting my moral responsibility. But Wittgenstein's need to escape marks his action as *heteronomous*: driven by necessity, by a (physical, emotional, mental) force independent of his free will, rather than autonomously chosen. In the later comments on cinema in Adorno's lectures on moral philosophy this sense of struggle is even more marked: we need to resist those 'processes that will transform us into what we are supposed to become and what we are making of ourselves in order to enable us to survive, and to ensure that we conform' (PMP 168). If these sentences sound strange, it is because Adorno insists that we do not simply need to resist pressures external to us, 'the processes that will transform us', but also our own efforts to survive: 'what we are making of ourselves'. The struggle for moral autonomy means not merely overcoming that which presses on us from without, but also a self-overcoming. Whether this is possible or even desirable is left as a somewhat open question.

FREEDOM AND SOCIETY

As we have already seen, for Adorno the idea of 'culture' implies a sense of something more than the mere self-preservation of human life: culture is the word we use to indicate those achievements which are not dictated by mere necessity. His idea of morality is similar. Morality names the possibility of acting in a way which is not determined by the compulsion of nature. In other words the question of morality is for Adorno a question of the possibility of freedom for the individual, of a free action which is compelled neither by biological or social needs. Up to this point, Adorno follows Kant. However he makes two qualifications of this argument. Firstly, following Hegel, he seeks to relate Kant's rather abstract attempt to deduce the possibility of morality and of freedom to the concrete situations in which individuals make such judgements. Secondly, following Nietzsche, he starts asking questions about the origins of morality. These questions both modify in significant ways the Kantian account: if Adorno had already stressed the harsh side of Kant, these both make morality seem even more extreme. The first sees the achievement of freedom as a matter not for the individual, but for society as a whole. Kant's question is incorrectly posed in isolating the possibility of morality from the network of social relations in which an individual is embedded, and in underplaying the blocks that network may place on the possibility of a moral action. The second is even more radical, since it questions the very desirability of the Kantian account of morality. If morality has a historical origin, can it any longer have a rational justification? Characteristically, these challenges to the basic account of morality we have outlined are rarely made explicit in Adorno's work, but are interwoven with critical analysis of actual social situations. The following discussion aims to disentangle them.

In *Minima Moralia* Adorno makes a passing aside: 'Free time remains the reflex-action to a production rhythm imposed heteronomously on the subject, compulsively maintained even in its weariest pauses' (MM 175). In a later essay called 'Free Time', originally a radio broadcast, Adorno expands on this argument at some length. What we see as the suspension of labour is mere respite from it. What we call 'free' time might be better expressed as spare time or recovery time. Our need to work undermines our ability to claim a legitimate autonomy. Even when we are not

97

working, our rest or relaxation is determined by the need to prepare for work, anticipate work, or simply to work again. Interestingly, this places Adorno into confrontation not only with the contemporary social world, but also with the Marxist revaluation of labour, as work which has transformed the world so far, and thus might transform it for the better. Adorno simply denies freedom: 'neither in their work nor in their consciousness are people freely in charge of themselves' (CM 167). What we call our 'free' time, through being a kind of licensed and temporary release from labour, only emphasizes our inability to stop working. His concern is that while so-called free time available to people is expanding, and the possibilities of further technological progress means that this might continue, 'the suspicion is unavoidable that free time is tending toward the opposite of its own concept and is becoming a parody of itself' (CM 168).

Having stated this theme, Adorno proceeds to explore it through a series of examples. As so often in his work, Adorno's comments suggest the slight detachment from reality on which his friend Lowenthal commented. Does he really believe that office life is such that if one returns from a holiday without a suntan, one's colleagues will not believe one has been away? Is he being serious in attacking DIY? However tempting to ascribe a biographical or psychological significance to Adorno's comments, we should resist. As in the case of his ban on visits to the cinema, he deliberately pushes an argument to the extreme: in this case to destroy the quietist sentiment that we work in order to enjoy ourselves in our spare time, which implies a certain amount of autonomy. Adorno is trying to force us into seeing things from the other side, in which our lives are determined by the need to work, and are therefore heteronomous. The idea of free time, like the idea of freedom itself, looks illusory from this angle. Certainly, Adorno's suggestions that the idea of free time is inextricably bound up with commerce are uncontroversial. He correctly identifies the tremendous potential of the 'leisure industry', and he correlates the idea of hobbies, as activities for one's spare time for which endless equipment must be acquired, with the development of an industry to satisfy such needs. The reversal of perspective which inverts the idea of free time into something rather more sinister brings into focus not the individual's autonomy from the social system, but the domination of the social system over the individual, and the extent to which our choices and options are all products of a totality over which we have little control. This is Adorno's somewhat melodramatic way of making the Hegelian point that, *contra* Kant, the possibility of individual freedom may in fact be rather limited by our participation in capitalist society.

This builds up into a wider sense of social unfreedom, which runs through much of Adorno's analysis of modern society. This is often uncomfortable to readers – and is intended to be – because we tend to take our own freedom of choice rather lightly, and Adorno's claim that more and more of our actions are compelled by social and commercial imperatives acting on us is something we are inclined to deny. We should not misunderstand Adorno. He seems to be saying that people simply have no freedom, and that what they take to be their decisions are not their own: the implication being that they are mindless automatons, while the philosopher can see the true nature of things. But this would go against Adorno's emphasis, as we saw in the last chapter, on culture as a horizon of knowledge and practices which we share, and in which the critic is also embedded. So to avoid claiming to have escaped the social world, and its illusions, and to be consistent in his arguments, Adorno's point must be rather that we cannot know the extent to which what we choose to do is the object of a free decision. Morality cannot be a fact: we can never assert that we have acted freely, morally, because we can never be sure that our actions have not been dictated or programmed by the social or biological imperatives from which morality claims to be a liberation. From the point of view of morality this is an attack on any claim to live a free and moral existence, but from another point of view it puts morality itself into question, by suggesting that to ask the question in these terms is inadequate. What use is an account of morality based on freedom from need, when so much of human life is driven by need?

Moreover, as in the case of Adorno's account of the culture industry, he never simply ascribes industry total domination over people's behaviour. The account of camping in 'Free Time' is an interesting example:

Camping, which was a favourite activity of the older Youth Movement, was a protest against the tedium and conventionalism of bourgeois life. One wanted to get out, in both senses of the word. Sleeping under the open sky meant having escaped house and family. After the death of the Youth Movement this need was taken up and institutionalized by the camping industry. It could not compel people to buy its tents and trailers, along with innumerable accessories, were there not some longing for such items in people already, but business functionalizes, extends and reproduces their need for freedom; what they want is being imposed upon them once again. (CM 170)

Note that Adorno does not deny the validity of people's experience: their instinctive need for freedom testifies from the subjective side to the social unfreedom which he is concerned to describe objectively. Notice too that this need is aligned with what we can now recognize as moral imperatives: escape from social pressures, 'the tedium and conventionalism of bourgeois life', and an overcoming of the familiar, of 'house and family'. Business does not implant the idea of escape, but 'functionalizes, extends and reproduces it': as in the case of culture, industry follows and distorts rather than leads. Indeed, business could not exploit people's needs so effectively if they were not responding to what was once a real need. It is also striking that the contrast Adorno draws is not between institutionalized camping and some romantic ideal of the wandering pedlar or minstrel, but with the Youth Movement of the early twentieth century, already a reaction against urban bourgeois life. The idea of camping can be deciphered not as a false copy of some authentic and free relation to the outdoors, but as the historical effacement of what was already a sign of a perceived loss. Adorno's suspicion of any claim to immediacy or spontaneity is determined by his acknowledgement that 'whatever is in the context of bourgeois delusion called nature, is merely the scar of social mutilation' (MM 95). The appeal of camping testifies to a debased and institutionalized impulse, which is itself an index of unfreedom, the sign of a felt lack.

In an interview broadcast seven days after his death, and more than twenty years after *Minima Moralia*, Adorno comments that 'the society in which we live is heteronomous, i.e., no one in contemporary society can really lead a life that is self-determined'.[7] Self-determination, the autonomy of moral rationality for which Kant argued, is impossible in the world today. It is on these grounds that Adorno can judge this a wrong life. However, it is important to keep an eye on the way Adorno's arguments work. If society has come to obstruct the freedom of the individual, is that because something has gone wrong with society, and it has turned from fostering autonomy to cancelling it, or is it rather the case that society and freedom have always been in conflict? What Adorno might be doing is presenting a critical account of that relation in order to emphasize that, as he puts it in his lectures on Moral Philosophy, 'it is not the task of moral philosophy to strive to reduce conflict to harmony' (PMP 144)? If this is indeed the case, then his apparent refutation of Kant's account of morality through an appeal to the experience of contemporary unfreedom would look less like a historical account of freedom's decline, and more like an attempt to sustain Kant's critical interrogation of the concept, through an insistence that morality is just not the sort of thing about which we might ever draw firm conclusions. Right living would be impossible not so much because society is somehow inherently evil, but because the nature of right and wrong is such that one can never confidently be said to have eclipsed the other.

Part of the resistance we may feel to Adorno's use of the idea of freedom is that the way we generally think about freedom has evolved to avoid precisely this kind of conflict: a tendency found not only in our everyday use of the term, but also in the predominant trends in liberal political theory. When we use the word 'freedom' we tend to mean either that no physical or legal limitations constrain us from acting according to our wishes, or looked at from the other side, that I have the legal or physical capacity to carry out my desired actions. In political terms this is the famous contrast between positive and negative liberties: liberty as a set of rights I hold as a citizen; liberty as a set of restrictions on what others, or the state, may impose upon me. Freedom in all these senses is closely tied to the idea of the individual. The individual holds rights or is protected from the infringement of his liberties. But there are grave problems with this account which Adorno's arguments can actually make reasonable sense of. The autonomy of the individual is simply presumed, rather than proved. Freedom describes the extent to which I am able to carry out what I take to be my freely chosen actions. The question of the extent to which my desires or beliefs have been chosen for me is simply left out of the equation, and thus the Kantian question of the validity of my actions – whether I act out of a sense of duty or not – cannot be raised. In which case the question of my real autonomy can never actually be posed. Moreover, by focusing on the individual agent, these accounts of freedom tie into the capitalist vision of the subject as buyer and seller of labour.

For Adorno, a moral philosophy which starts from the individual is already falsely assuming their autonomy: abstracting them from the social environment on which they are dependent. No account of morality which neglects the extent to which people are immersed in a concrete historical world will be able to do anything but repeat the tendency to pit the individual against the world. But this autonomy, in setting the individual against the social world, is illusory: it masks real needs, and real involvement with others. By rejecting our mutual interdependence on other human beings, and on the natural environment which supports us, morality becomes merely a justification for the continuation of the war of all against all which Adorno, following Hobbes, sees as the state of nature. A liberal moral philosophy which starts from man as an autonomous individual is simply no moral philosophy at all, because morality is one of those aspects of culture which enable us to suspend such violence. Adorno follows an alternative tradition, best exemplified in the work of Rousseau and Hegel, for whom freedom for one is meaningless without freedom for the whole. The antipathy of the individual to a social order which he feels imposes itself against him is a consequence of the unreconciled nature of society, equally enacted in the philosophical antinomy of subject and object. So Adorno does not deny the subjective experience of alienation, of being set against a social totality which does not seem to correspond to one's interests or desires. Rather, both liberal political thought – of which Kant becomes the example – and individual experience in bourgeois society have to be explained, not as a moment to be resolved into a higher synthesis, but as an insurpassable problem.

Adorno's most explicit account of freedom, given in *Negative Dialectics*, goes something like this. Freedom is partially activated in the transition from a feudal or absolutist to a bourgeois society. The individual gains a degree of autonomy in being able to determine his own actions, and in buying and selling his or her goods or labour power. However freedom in a market society is in these terms submission to the market. The freedom of the individual is only partial, remaining dependent on economic needs. Freedom fails to live up to its promise of reconciliation between the individual and society: a promise which allows us to criticize not only social unfreedom, but also the partial freedom hypostatized in liberal philosophies which justify the freedom of the individual. The authoritarian overtones of Kant's insistence on moral autonomy as submission to, or respect for the law, derive from the experience of such laws as external to the individual. This leads to a complicated situation: 'society is in the wrong against the individual in its general claims, but it is also in the right against him, since the social principle of unreflected self-preservation . . . is hypostatized in the individual' (ND 283). To denounce the individual in the name of social conformism would be to enforce unfreedom; to denounce society in the name of the individual would be to sustain not just a one-sided view, but to threaten to abolish freedom altogether, in returning to a state of nature. The discussion of freedom in *Negative Dialectics* does not seek to directly resolve this situation. An acknowledgement of the subjective experience of it is juxtaposed with historical and psychological models of its development; philosophical analysis of the objective contradictions of the concept of freedom itself; and critical analysis of the historical and philosophical development of the concepts in failed philosophies of freedom.

Does Adorno believe in freedom? As in the case of culture in the preceding chapter, this is not a question we can answer in any straightforward fashion. Adorno believes that our idea of freedom is part of the problem, since it one-sidedly separates the individual from their real dependence on nature and on society. It misrepresents the individual as autonomous. However, Kant's rather hardline account of moral philosophy, particularly when taken to its extreme, need not serve as a justification for the status quo, but through its stress on overcoming can act as a stimulus for change. In pushing Kant's thinking to its limit, Adorno's exposition can be seen as both a fulfilment of moral philosophy and its destruction. Negative dialectic, attacks unfreedom in the name of freedom, but then attacks freedom in terms of its own history. Adorno seems to conclude that self-determination, the autonomy of moral rationality for which Kant argued, is impossible in the world today: but this is more a reflection of his refusal to assume that it *is* possible: critical thought must leave this an open question.

DIALECTIC OF ENLIGHTENMENT

In 1784 a newspaper approached Kant for a contribution to a survey they were running of answers to the question 'What is Enlightenment?'. Kant's response has become famous: 'Enlightenment is the human being's emergence from his self-incurred minority.

Minority is the inability to make use of one's own understanding without direction from another.'[8] This answer expresses Kant's confidence in the power of reason to liberate humanity from superstition, and the future prospects of the rational autonomy which the possibility of aesthetic and moral judgements proves to exist. What Kant does not do is to identify 'Enlightenment' with a particular time and place: he does not mention an 'age of Enlightenment' in the way historians and scholars are sometimes tempted to. At a polar opposite to Kant's optimism lies the proposal, made by the modern moral philosopher Alasdair MacIntyre in his book *After Virtue*, that we understand the era of Enlightenment as the scene of a catastrophe that has bequeathed the modern world only fragmentary remains of previously coherent conceptions of morality. Adorno's position lies somewhere in between. He cannot share Kant's optimism, but his account of morality remains profoundly Kantian.

The extent to which this is the case can be seen in the ways in which Adorno remains faithful to the project of Kantian critical philosophy. In particular, Adorno's refusal to derive the failings of modern moral life from historical premises, in the way MacIntyre does, shows the basic continuity between his own thought and Kant's: rather than presume that the way we think can be understood as a reflection of the historical circumstances in which we think, both Kant and Adorno recognize that history is itself an *idea*. An argument which claims to know what history is and proceeds to explain questions of morality or knowledge on that basis is simply circular. In order to break out of this circle Kant, and Adorno follows him in this, demands a critical philosophy, by which he means a philosophy which reflects on the possibility of rational understanding, rather than simply assuming that empirical knowledge (for example, of history) is possible. For Adorno, Kant's answers are simply not critical *enough*: and he sees himself not as rejecting Kant, but as making critical philosophy even more critical.

This may not be immediately obvious. There are three reasons. The first is that the two sources of Adorno's major criticisms of the Kantian account of morality, Hegel and Nietzsche, can both be easily mistaken for historicist thinkers – indeed MacIntyre sometimes appears as an unwieldy combination of the two. The second is that, as we have seen, Adorno does indeed argue that empirical – social, historical – conditions operate as limits on the possibility of morality. This claim appears to be empirical or historical rather than critical. Thirdly, *Dialectic of Enlightenment* has every appearance of being primarily historical. Because to read *Dialectic of Enlightenment* as privileging historical explanation over critical reasoning completely abolishes the power of much of its argument, this is rather a large flaw. So while in this section I wish to draw on the book to extend my account of Adorno's moral thought, I will also show why we need to be rather wary.

The story which *Dialectic of Enlightenment* appears to be telling is rather a neat one. Kant's faith in Enlightenment, in the progressive liberation of mankind from superstition, is wrong. Reason, which Kant takes to be the foundation of free and autonomous existence, is in fact the opposite: a manifestation of mankind's will to dominate nature. In seeking to free himself from nature, man forgets his own dependence on and participation in the natural world. As we have already seen Adorno argue, man believes reason sets him apart from the animals. Because this serves to justify their exploitation by man, and thus man's continuing participation in the violence and anarchy of nature, reason turns out to be not the motor of man's liberation, but only a further means of his enslavement. From this comes Adorno and Horkheimer's famous starting point: 'Enlightenment, understood in the widest sense as the advance of thought, has always aimed at liberating human beings from fear and installing them as masters. Yet the wholly enlightened earth is radiant with triumphant calamity' (DE 1). Criticism of Kant's faith in Enlightenment is as old as that faith itself, and Adorno and Horkheimer draw on an array of the most gloomy and pessimistic thinkers to elaborate their case.

Most notoriously, by synthesizing Freud and Nietzsche, they argue for a kind of pseudo-individuality coextensive with the historical emergence of the bourgeois class in Europe. Following Nietzsche, they proceed genealogically: they undercut claims made on behalf of modern values by showing them to be the product of particular violent historical developments forgotten in the modern use of the concept. So they argue that reason is not an intrinsic human capacity but the result of the development of the instinct for self-preservation. The success of reason at continuing to ensure man's survival leads man to forget that reason is a natural phenomenon, and to hypostatize both reason and man as somehow higher than the rest of the world on which they act. Drawing on Freud they claim that man's successful survival in the bourgeois commercial world depends on the development of the ego, a strength of character which depends on shutting out the rest of the social world, and derives individuality or personality from domination.

Here Adorno rejoins Nietzsche. In his work *On the Genealogy of Morality*, Nietzsche equates morality with cruelty, and seeks to radically dethrone the supremacy of moral concepts by arguing that they have only developed in order to further the struggle of man against man. In particular he castigates the 'slave morality' (broadly: modern liberal philosophy and thought) for elevating the idea of equality to a supreme value. Closely linked to his criticisms of modern society, Nietzsche sees this as a levelling of all hierarchies and an inability to tell what things are truly worth. Nietzsche reserves particular scorn for Kant. His philosophy 'smells of cruelty'; it represents the overbearing attempt to find indisputable grounds for one account of morality, designed to replace the direct rule of the monarch with the indirect rule of the moral law, perfectly internalized by each subject. There are two important ideas at work here: the first is that since the moral law has a historical origin, how can it be universally binding?; the second is that morality is not other-worldly, but bound up in man's domination of nature, and the conflicts between men. Ultimately, for Nietzsche, the equality of men celebrated by the moral law derives from the needs of merchants to rank and evaluate products: equality is the loss of singularity, it is the reduction of my freedom, my individuality and the submission to a formal law of equivalence, deriving from the commercial world. In Marxist terms, morality serves to justify and make natural a system in which I am only valued in terms of my labour power, and in which men are as disposable or fungible as commodities. The bourgeois principle of the sacred value of individuality or subjectivity is merely an ideological counter to this real lack of substance in a moral and social environment shaped by the principle of exchange.

Nietzsche's attack on Kant is brutal. However, it is far from unprecedented, and readers of Kant had been arguing since at least Hegel that his account of morality was fatally one-sided, in leaving historical questions out of consideration. Hegel in particular suggests that Kant's account of morality takes no account of the limitations which social conditions might place on the individual's capacity to act morally. Freedom, which would enable me to act morally, to live a right life, may simply not be a possibility in some situations. Capitalism, and the domination of the exchange principle, render autonomy impossible. Adorno follows closely these Hegelian and Nietzschean criticisms of Kant. This is what lends his work on moral philosophy its dialectical character: with Kant and against Kant at the same time. Nietzsche's genealogy is intended as a ground-clearing exercise, a destructive overturning of conventional values in order to prepare the way for something new. The same might be said of Adorno. As we have seen he is not interested in dismissing Kantian morality out of hand, but in exaggerating it to the point where it becomes self-critical, i.e. critical of its own pretensions to be more than mere nature, to allow it to open onto the possibility of acknowledging that morality is not grounded in reason.

The task of *Dialectic of Enlightenment*, were it to be carried through to the creation of a critical theory, rather than being deliberately left in the form of a set of Philosophical Fragments, as the important subtitle reminds us, would be to synthesize psychological, historical and anthropological accounts to produce a single natural-history of reason. Such a history would trace the emergence of reason as a survival mechanism; the invention of the autonomous individual; the progress of Enlightenment as the development of reason's domination over nature which contradicts its claim to have escaped nature. The adaptation of the ego – which is designed to resist the hold of society over the individual – becomes a prison, which masks the actual dependence of the subject on the world, and falsely reifies reason as an autonomous force. Were they to complete this project, Adorno and Horkheimer would have made audacious claims, which would lead them to characterize reason as a natural phenomenon which also transcended nature. As it is, in its incomplete form, this transcendence of nature by reason, man's claim to have escaped the realm of necessity and reached the possibility of free autonomous action, is not denied but suspended. It can only be the object of speculative thinking, since it cannot be known for sure. Because this is above all a question of the possibility of progress as such, morality becomes a matter of philosophy of history – i.e. the enquiry as to whether history has a meaning, rather than being the continuous blind pursuit of self-preservation and survival. The chance of history happening, of progress being made, is what needs to be proved, not assumed.

But *Dialectic of Enlightenment* remains in fragmentary form. Three essays explore the idea of Enlightenment itself, the culture industry and anti-Semitism. Two further essays, marked as 'Excurses' (side investigations), examine Odysseus as a prototype bourgeois individualist, whose cunning is a matter of an adaptation of reason to survive over his environment, and the relationship between morality and Enlightenment. The book concludes with some shorter fragments, which anticipate the mode of *Minima Moralia* but seem to be mostly scraps which could not be worked into the larger essays. The explicit concern to treat Enlightenment and myth in the context of philosophy as a whole, and not just modern philosophy, should be enough to tell us that this is not a history of the modern capitalist world. In fact, it is more of an attack on the tools which might offer such a history than it is a history of its own. Because it is reason which must process and analyse our knowledge about the world, the fact that reason itself cannot be taken for an independent and neutral instrument, but part and parcel of our success in adapting to the world, or of our submission to the natural instinct to dominate it and our failure to transcend mere need.

This gives us a more systematic presentation of the conceptual constriction which accounts for the apparent strangeness of much of Adorno's work. To understand the world means relating thought to history, and without freezing either: an eternal and unchanging world to be manipulated by an invincible thought. The two interact: our consideration of one or the other can only be mediated. But to be able to ask how history affects us, and what history is, we would need to be able to settle on a fixed and definitive idea of epistemology, of the relationship between knowledge and reason. But this understanding is what the movement of history denies us. So the mediation of the two aspects of the world, of history and reason, is not a mere formula. It is a challenge, a crisis of both objective knowing and of historical existence. What we have already learnt about freedom, about the strange moral imperative of thought in Adorno, can show us this in a different light. Because Adorno applies epistemological cautions to the way we think about history, we can't see history as somehow the master narrative of his whole project. If Adorno started off with a fixed and determined idea of history, he would be effectively introducing unfreedom, establishing history as a necessary rather than contingent and malleable form. Equally, to see the world as historical, as constructed, can only be a moral decision: it means not to resign oneself to mere affirmation of what is. So Adorno must see philosophy – epistemology – within its context, but also as an attempt to come to terms with its context: not by trying to master it (subordinate or exhaust it) by reducing it to a context, but by seeking to open philosophy up to its context again (which it has

generally sought to cut off). These three perspectives: history, epistemology and moral questions are intertwined. We will return to the
problems of enlightenment's relation to myth in the fourth chapter,
when we will examine the other (and dialectically necessary) half of
the argument, that myth must already be enlightenment. Here
however, I want to stress the consequences of the arguments about
enlightenment for the way we think about philosophy and reason in
their relationship to history. For one way of understanding all
enlightenment, in its claim to distinguish itself from myth, would be
as dependent on a philosophy of history. However much logical or
formal modes of argument claim to be neutral historically, or purely
empirical, they carry with them a claim to be not just true to the
world of experience, but 'truer' than other forms. On this claim rests
not only their self-definition but also their value. Science in this sense
is indeed what makes the alteration and construction of the world
possible. It would be entirely self-defeating to dismiss the claim to be
able to specify such a situation with precision and clarity. To admit
that reason is not secure from unreason is not to commit a 'perfor-
mative contradiction': thought can only be convicted of such from a
neutral, ahistorical, purely logical vantage point, precisely that which
is unavailable.

The genealogy of morals which Adorno and Horkheimer under-
take in *Dialectic of Enlightenment* does not depend on a claim to be
an accurate depiction of how things happened: it is directed above all
at the possibility of change in the present, by sharpening our sense of
the contradictions between freedom and society. Both society and the
way we think about morality need to be changed. Only once we recognize that their current relationship is at an impasse, and that the
only way out is *through*, are we approaching the position Adorno
shares with Horkheimer. So as a provisional guide to the task that
Dialectic of Enlightenment undertakes, we might say that it seeks to
try and dissolve, through its telling, the single history which links the
rise of modern capitalism to the failure or impotence of bourgeois
philosophy and morals. We can see that there is a parallel here to the
problem of freedom. Freedom turns into unfreedom since its very
claim to autonomy and self-determination turns out to rest on a
denial of mediation and dependence: thought's inextricable connection to the world. Similarly, enlightenment cannot simply be opposed
to myth, which it claims to supersede, but to which it stands in a much
more complex and ambivalent relation.

THE MORALITY OF THINKING

One way of thinking about Adorno's work is to see it as an attempt to develop a way of thinking which might negotiate with what must remain thought's own blindspots. *Dialectic of Enlightenment* shows that it is possible to consider the development of man's rational faculty not as a miraculous and God-given sign of man's election over the beasts of the earth, but as an evolutionary advantage which has made man sovereign not by right, but through an increase in his might. Adorno's commitment to materialism might be taken as a passionate concern with the extent to which the perception of man as a free and autonomous agent acting in the world is merely the reflex to man's blindness to his own true motivations. History, culture, morality: these may all turn out to be illusions spun, not merely to disguise our animal natures from ourselves, but to better organize and refine the capacity of the species for destruction. The gamble of Adorno's thought is that the development of reason is not, or is not only, a merely technical development. In other words, that reason might make something like progress possible. But this can only be achieved if reason can sustain the critical impulse which places its own apparent freedom and autonomy under suspicion. As soon as we assume that freedom is possible, we are acting in conformity to a particular conception of the world, and have condemned ourselves to unfreedom.

The difficulties of Adorno's thinking, and of its presentation, are thus all dictated as a response to what one fragment of *Minima Moralia* names 'the morality of thinking' (MM 73–5). This is the demand that reason should try to do two things at once. On the one hand to allow the world as it is to speak: reason must efface itself before the object of thought, rather than trying to integrate it into its plans and schemes. This would mean a non-instrumental knowledge of reality, a relationship of thought to the world which was no longer the manifestation of science as will to power, in which the world is anatomized in order to be better controlled and manipulated by reason. This process is not an addition but begins at the very heart of rational thought, in the relationship between concepts and the world. On the Kantian model, we recognize and organize our perceptions of the things we encounter in the world by subsuming them under concepts. Adorno protests that this act of knowing is violent, in equating individual and particular objects, by imposing subjective categories on them. In *Dialectic of Enlightenment* Adorno and Horkheimer remark that 'in the world of mass production, stereotypes replace intellectual categories. Judgement is no longer based on a real act of synthesis but on blind subsumption' (DE 166–7). The distinction between judgement and subsumption is that between a mental process which reduces objects to fit into particular classes, and that in which a genuine judgement is made, and the object is treated as individual. Note that this is directly analogous to the importance of certain kinds of musical form to Adorno; and that the centrality of both aesthetic and moral judgement to Adorno, following Kant, is that if such judgements were possible, our freedom would be proven.

This suspicion of concepts must obviously cause great problems for Adorno, since he recognizes no other form of rigorous thought. As he argues in *Negative Dialectic*, philosophy must 'strive, by way of the concept, to transcend the concept' (ND 15). The impulse behind this is a moral one: like Kantian morality, which depends on something like a self-overcoming, so thinking needs to challenge and resist its own operations. To the extent that it succeeds in doing so, it affirms its own freedom, and that of the world. This dictates the other obligation of the morality of thinking: never to forget the subjective nature of thought. As soon as we imagine that we have bypassed the difficulties of reason, and apprehended the world as it is, we falsely imagine we have achieved an unmediated possession of the object. Adorno's stress on mediation, and on the dialectical relation between subject and object, is intended to underline that there is no unreflected, unmediated access to reality.

The consequences of this are considerable. If in his criticisms of society and of the limits of rationalist thought Adorno can seem to be repeating the positions of the Romantic reaction to eighteenth-century thought, in his account of reason and nature it is possible to draw a distinction. Romantic thought was premised on the reconciliation of subject and object, on the construction of a philosophical position from which man could be seen as part of nature. The world was to be apprehended as a unity, in which both man and the natural world had their place. This idea of reconciliation is rejected in Adorno's work, which prefers to understand the relation between man and nature not in terms of a possible synthesis, but in terms of a continuing antagonism. Romantic thought urges the priority of unity over diversity, of the whole over its parts. The Romantic reaction against mechanism means that the world is either treated *as* God, or as infused with purpose and destiny. Such an account of man's place in the world would be teleological, in assuming a development from lower to higher, and thus depend on an idea of progress. For all these reasons, this kind of reconciliation is anathema to Adorno, for whom the idea of purpose or meaning in the world is precisely what may not be taken for granted, and for whom the only progress has been the development of technological means of domination over the world.

Adorno indicts reason for its destruction of nature; but also invokes something like a natural history of reason to account for its destructive tendencies. To do so relies on the power of reason. Autonomous reason can only overcome its own natural history, not by somehow rejecting rationality, by abolishing itself or by simply embracing its opposite, nature, but by seeking to admit nature into reason, admitting its always heteronomous involvement with the natural world. In other words, we must be careful not to misunderstand Adorno as simply a philosopher of *either* nature or reason. Both Adorno's interest in dialectics, and thus in the inseparable contamination of apparently opposing concepts, and his insistence on mediation, on the unavailability of some spontaneous or free alternative to the perspective of human reason, would suggest that just as reason turns out to be a continuation of nature's bloody fight for survival, so nature must turn out to be a retrospective fantasy of the rational mind: there can be no simple escape from one to the other. Where Rousseau saw an insuperable divide between nature and culture, which inaugurates both the benefits and the losses of life within society, Adorno sees in society as it is merely the continuation of the Hobbesian idea of nature as the war of all against all. To seek to shrug off the rationalism that has distorted the world would also be to give up those elements in it which alone form a bulwark against pure barbarism, to give up on the possibility of redemption within culture.

As so often, we find Adorno at the limits of what a strict materialism can achieve. A wholly mechanistic account of the development of man would have to include a natural history of reason: to account for the development of the rational faculties as an extension of man's natural instinct for self-preservation. Reasoning gives man a competitive advantage over other animals. But it leads man to hypostatize reason, and indeed his own status. Once man sees himself as different from the animals, they have become reduced to objects. The motor for this is man's assumption of his difference. If we hold to a strictly mechanical genealogy of morality, as Nietzsche offers, we see that good and bad, moral categories are equally functional rather than absolute, that they organize and provide hierarchies within society. Adorno resists this deterministic conclusion by seeing in reason the possibility of something other than domination. The fact that reason can reflect on its own nature, the possibility that we can understand that reason is an outcome of nature, also allows for the possibility of going against nature. Reason means we have the chance of going against our instincts and desires. As Adorno argues in his lectures on moral philosophy, 'the truth is that we are no longer simply a piece of nature from the moment we recognize that we are a piece of nature' (PMP 103). Or as he rephrases it: 'by virtue of that fact (of being able to observe "I myself am a part of nature") the human subject is liberated from the blind pursuit of natural ends and becomes capable of alternative actions' (PMP 103). Man's emancipation from nature through reason leads him into responsibility and the difficulties of moral philosophy.

Once we have entered into philosophy, into reflection, and into language, we finally have a chance of affirming freedom. However, this can only be achieved through the critical negation of unfreedom, through our tangled recognition of the failure of reason to deliver us from our natural condition. This is why Adorno's dialectic is negative. So our task is not to perfect reason, but to criticize it; not to achieve morality, but to show how when we imagine we have lived rightly, we have not. This becomes an insistence on our inevitable guilt. As soon as we start to think, we subsume particulars under concepts: we negate the individuality of the particular object in the generality of the concept. This is part of the same process which leads us to insist on our illusory autonomy, and to hypostatize reason as that which divides us from the animals.

Inevitably, Adorno's best examples come back to the question of the animal. They fill the role of the exemplary object, in its resistance to conceptual appropriation: 'In existing without any purpose recognizable to men, animals hold out, as if for expression, their own names, utterly impossible to exchange. This makes them so beloved of children, their contemplation so blissful. I am a rhinoceros signifies the shape of the rhinoceros' (MM 228). 'The exploitation and maltreatment of animals' is the 'most obvious and tangible expression' of the fact that 'the establishment of total rationality as the supreme objective principle of mankind might well spell the continuation of . . . blind domination of nature' (PMP 145). The animals we oppress include ourselves; and morality is one of the vehicles through which such oppression takes place. Hence, no doubt, its smell of cruelty. But morality, like rationality, is also an opportunity for something else to happen, for the chance of establishing another, non-coercive, relationship to the world. The morality of thinking requires that we seek to explore such a possibility through the self-criticism of reason. Self-criticism means an insistence on guilt: on the inevitable failure of thought to do justice to the world, by its violent subsumption of the particular under the general – which lies at the heart of conceptualization itself. Crucially for the political dimensions of Adorno's work, in the attempt to transform society, to make freedom actual, 'concepts alone can achieve what the concept prevents' (ND 53). This determines Adorno's insistence that it is not action, but thought which will save us: 'The spell that binds us today consists not least in the fact that it ceaselessly urges people to take *action* that they *believe* will break the spell; and that it prevents the *reflection* on themselves and the circumstances that might *really* break it' (MCP 126).

LIVING WITH GUILT

In terms of practical philosophy – understanding how we might make difficult moral judgements in our everyday life – Adorno's work may seem oppressively absolute. If we take at face value the claim that in 'wrong life' right living is impossible, that the overwhelming totality of social forces denies us freedom and therefore the very possibility of moral autonomy, we might be tempted to draw the conclusion that we should not even try to live a good life, since we are doomed to fail. But the very fact of being able to state this case must mean that the free use of reason is still to some extent possible, however attenuated. It is just this gap between the domination of the social whole and the promises of culture – freedom, truth, the good – in which Adorno's thought operates. This unreconciled state of being-between can be understood in historical terms as one of the inexorable dilemmas of modernity. However such a diagnosis tends to imply either a prior state of grace or a possible future state of perfection: better to understand it as an epistemological condition. Thought will never be able to do justice to the world, since the subsumption of the particular under the concept effaces its individuality and renders things merely equivalent: but this does not mean we should stop thinking. Equally, our inevitable failure to achieve autonomy – to make a free moral decision in Adorno's Kantian terms – does not mean that we should stop trying. Rather, like our epistemology, our moral philosophy needs to become reflexive and self-critical. Only prolonged and careful attention to the limits of what a rational account of morality can achieve will allow for the possibility – and nothing is less certain than its success – of doing more than merely perpetuating man's drive to dominate nature.

In theoretical terms, Adorno's arguments have some clear consequences for how we think about moral philosophy. His suspicion of reason leads him to reject the characteristic modern quest to find a rational ground for morality. The intervention of conceptual thought immediately effaces the urgency of the moral decision: 'as soon as one attempts to provide a logical foundation for a proposition such as that one should not torture, one becomes embroiled in a bad infinity' (MCP 15). There is an irreducible non-rational element in morality: it exceeds our reasoned calculations as to what is the right thing to do. This does not make morality wholly irrational, but suggests that just as enlightenment turns into myth, so justice cannot be conceived as a rational calculating machine, except at the cost of forgetting the non-rational moments from which our moral impulses derive: sympathy, disgust. This also means that Adorno no longer looks to a moral theory to resolve practical dilemmas. His aporetic approach to moral philosophy begins from the premise that there may simply be no philosophical or theoretical way to decide between two competing moral claims. In the wrong life, there can be no right living. Morality is not a matter of making the right choice, as of living with the awareness that no right choice is possible.

Adorno devoted his lecture of 23 July 1963 to a discussion of Ibsen's *The Wild Duck* in an attempt to give a more concrete example of the problems of morality with which he had been dazzling his audience since the start of May. The central theme of the play is the destruction of an innocent life as the consequence of one man's quest for purity. The play traces the consequences of the actions of Gregers Werle, whose belief that no-one should live under false pretences leads him to explain to an old friend, Hialmat Ekdal, that Ekdal's wife has previously been Werle's father's mistress, and that the child Ekdal thinks is his may not be, initiating the tragic chain of events. The moral claim of Werle's actions are undeniable: Adorno identifies him with the categorical imperative, and certainly Kant argued that there was no situation in which a lie could be justified. But Ibsen's sympathies are divided, and he shows that owing to circumstances, had the young woman revealed her situation she would have been rejected by her suitor and ostracized by the community. Moreover, although her husband is a feckless dreamer who depends on her for his livelihood as well as the domestic arrangements, their family life is portrayed in touching, if slightly pathetic terms. Ibsen seems to suggest that there is right on both sides; and on neither. Werle may be morally correct, but the price is an inhuman thoughtlessness for others and a life of exile from the comforts of the community. The life of the Ekdal family is cosy and domestic, but at the price of any claim to virtue.

Just as Ibsen *dramatizes* this irreconcilable antagonism, so Adorno's moral thought has a dialectical, dialogical quality. The centrality of mediation in Adorno's work might also be taken as an indication that there his view of morality is cast in shades of grey, rather than black and white. However, Ibsen's work also focuses one other key issue. Werle links moral action to truth; the cynical character Relling argues that it is better for people to have what he calls 'life lies', false beliefs which help them evade reality. The play as a whole seems undecided. Just as myth and enlightenment are hopelessly intertwined, so we might read Adorno not as opposing the truth of critical philosophy to the saving illusion of the cinema, but as showing the two poles to be inextricably imbricated in one another. For the co-author of *Dialectic of Enlightenment*, reason cannot be the answer, but there can be no answer without reason. Existence will always be a cause for guilt; in moral terms I can never be out of debt. But Adorno also identifies morality as more than a little inhuman.

At the conclusion of his discussion of freedom in *Negative Dialectics*, Adorno adds the following cryptic gloss on the impossibility of living right in wrong life, and perhaps inevitably, returns to the example of the animal to make his point:

> In the socialized society, no individual is capable of the morality that is a social demand but would be a reality only in a free society . . . But the individual is left with no more than the morality for which Kantian ethics – which accords affection, not respect, to animals – can muster only disdain: to try to live so that one may believe himself to have been a good animal. (ND 299)

In distinguishing humans from animals, as in distinguishing the natural from the rational impulses within man, bourgeois morality ends up reinventing violent domination over nature, including one's own. The idea of the 'good animal' must be paradoxical within a morality which attributes 'right' to reason and makes morality the definition of the human. To live as a 'good animal' would be to aspire to the impossible: to accommodate the heteronomous within one's perceived autonomy, to accept that 'countless moments of external – notably social – reality invade the decisions designated by the words "will" and "freedom"' (ND 213). This means accepting that there will always be an antagonism between my power to do the right thing and the situation which I face, and that if I will always be guilty of things which were beyond my power to alter, there are perhaps other principles against which I might measure my duty. If duty should not be allowed to wholly overcome simple somatic pleasures – if the desire for happiness is *like* reason in being an aspect of man's animal nature, perhaps a trip to the cinema would not be totally out of the question. But what Adorno insists is that we should never forget that the price of such accommodation is also the relaxation of our critical vigilance, and the abnegation of our duty.

CHAPTER 4

PHILOSOPHY AND HISTORY

Philosophy has the curious characteristic that, although itself entrapped, locked inside the glasshouse of our constitution and our language, it is nevertheless able constantly to think beyond itself and its limits, to think itself through the walls of its glasshouse. And this thinking beyond itself, into openness – that, precisely, is metaphysics.

(MCP 68)

If thought is not measured by the extremity that eludes the concept, it is from the outset in the nature of the musical accompaniment with which the SS liked to drown out the screams of its victims.

(ND 365)

In 1969 Adorno and Horkheimer finally bowed to growing pressure and republished their by then notorious collaborative work *Dialectic of Enlightenment*. First distributed in a limited edition to a select group of sympathetic intellectuals in 1944, the book had only been made publicly available in 1947 when it was published in Amsterdam. Adorno and Horkheimer had been reluctant to agree to a reprint. Horkheimer in particular feared that it would be handing ammunition to their political opponents and in 1961 had refused permission for a proposed German second edition, although he did authorize an Italian translation at around this time. The authors were now prominent figures in West German cultural life and they anticipated a much wider audience than the small group of initiates for whom the first draft had been prepared during their years of exile in the United States, in the shadow of the Second World War and of the Nazi regime. As their colleague Friedrich Pollock warned them, their original language was somewhat 'unguarded'; indeed he judged that the text was simply not suitable for 'mass circulation'.[1] Indeed, certain subtle changes had been made for the Italian edition, only to be subject to detailed and angry scrutiny by radical leftists in Germany, sensing a betrayal or a retreat from earlier and more directly revolutionary positions.[2] But on the politicized and militant Frankfurt University campus of the 1960s unauthorized copies of *Dialectic of Enlightenment* were circulating widely amongst the students, finally provoking Horkheimer to agree to formal republication. The new German edition appeared in the year that Adorno died.

That the dissemination of a work of social and moral philosophy should be subject to political scrutiny is not perhaps surprising. Those branches of philosophy which seek to understand or even to intervene in history necessarily find themselves open to revision in the light of subsequent developments. A logician may wish to revise their earlier work in the light of their own subsequent insights, or of criticisms offered by other philosophers; but for a moral or political thinker, it is often history itself which passes judgement. The first edition of *Dialectic of Enlightenment* implies that a revolutionary transformation is the only answer to the apparent triumph of fascism in Europe; but after nearly twenty years of involvement in the democratic reconstruction of West German life, and confronted with the evident unfreedom of the Soviet Bloc, Adorno and Horkheimer are rather more circumspect about political radicalism than a younger generation who had not lived through the events of the 1930s and 1940s.

Yet the fact that a book written in one context may look rather different in another is not an accidental inconvenience for Adorno and Horkheimer: as they stress, it is an aspect of the fundamental problem with which their work is concerned. In the preface to the revised edition, Adorno and Horkheimer remark that while some of their ideas seem 'timely', they 'do not stand by everything we said in the book in its original form. That would be incompatible with a theory which attributes a temporal core to truth instead of contrasting truth as something invariable with the movement of history' (DE xi). This is a telling comment. It links a justification of their right to make such alterations as seem politically expedient with a central aspect of their philosophical position. Philosophy is sometimes conceived as an enquiry into those features of the world which do not change: truths about human nature, beauty, or what might constitute a good life; or rules whose validity is to be judged by their internal consistency (their logic) rather than by their conformity with the

temporal and material world. But for the strand of materialist thinking to which Adorno and Horkheimer belong, variation is more fundamental than stability: it is unending change rather than eternal
order with which philosophy must come to terms. So for Adorno,
philosophy and history are intimately connected. It is a lesson he had
learnt from his friend Walter Benjamin, who had himself derived it
from his reading of Nietzsche. When Adorno underlines his debt to
Nietzsche in his lectures on *Moral Philosophy* (PMP 172) he has in
mind, I think, what he calls in his tribute to Benjamin 'the later
Nietzsche's critical insight that truth is not identical within a timeless
universal, but rather that it is solely the historical which yields the
figure of the absolute' (P 231). Or in his lectures on *Metaphysics*:
'truth has a temporal core', which Adorno identifies as central to his
use of the concept of mediation (MCP 45). These are complicated
ways of saying something quite simple; but the consequences are far
from obvious, and the task of this final chapter will be explain and
analyse this crucial aspect of Adorno's thought.

To see philosophy and history as intimately linked is not in itself an
unusual position for a twentieth-century thinker: in fact it's probably
fair to say that some form of this thesis remains dominant in the
humanities. This presents the main difficulty for an examination of
Adorno's take on this relationship: his views look broadly similar to
a number of less sophisticated positions, while in fact entailing a total
rejection of them. Failure to distinguish properly between them has
been responsible for most of the misreadings of Adorno common in
non-technical accounts of his work. The extent of this difficulty in
turn underlines what I take to be the contemporary significance of
Adorno's thought: that even if we do not wholly accept the solution
proposed by Adorno, his diagnosis of the problem faced by critical
thought today seems irreproachable.

Particularly in the English-speaking world where twentieth-
century philosophy has been predominantly based on an analytic
model, there has been little critical safeguard against a broadly positivist view of the world, whose prestige derives largely from the
success of the natural sciences. But in Adorno's eyes positivism is a
reconciliation with the world as it is, rather than its critical destruction. Although the humanities have stayed in closer touch with the
idea of criticism, the eclipse of critical philosophy as a founding discipline by the historical and cultural sciences leads to a set of related
problems: if cultural phenomena are understood to be relative to a

particular historical context, if truth becomes merely a matter of belief, critical thought is replaced by the cataloguing of alternative myths about the world. Adorno's rejection of the idea that a sociological account of modernity can tell us how we came to be in our contemporary predicament is exemplary. Since both the idea of modernity and the principles of sociology must themselves be part of that very predicament, on what grounds are we to trust this account rather than any other? The idea of enlightenment, of our ever increasing knowledge of the world as it is, rapidly turns to myth. Or to put this in grander terms, once philosophy, which claims to be able to tell the difference between truth and mere opinion, accepts that truth is variable, because historical, it enters into crisis. What is unique and complex about Adorno's work is the insistence that accepting the historicity of truth need not mean surrendering to irrationalism. But this means refusing to back away from the crisis of philosophy.

This chapter could have been placed earlier on in the book; there were two reasons why I chose not to. Firstly, I wanted to avoid giving the impression that Adorno's work has a fundamental methodology. Although they echo and reflect his understanding of the relationship between philosophy and history, Adorno's analyses of art and morality are not derivative of a particular philosophy of history: his positions in all three areas arise from the attempt to come to terms with problems specific to each field, rather than being based on categories imported from outside. Secondly, I am aware that these concerns may well be more abstract, and therefore less easy to grasp, than others: in which case, the links to positions we have already examined will help illuminate the argument.

The first section, as in previous chapters, faces up to the most perplexing aspect of Adorno's work in this area. The problem is similar to that facing us in examining Adorno's writings on art and on morality: what seems to be the extreme negativity of identifying history with disaster, typified in Adorno's comments on the impossibility of poetry after Auschwitz. As in earlier chapters we need to understand these claims not as conclusions drawn from a philosophy of history, but the result of a critical and epistemological questioning of the possibility of speaking about history in the first place: indeed, it may be somewhat startling to discover that Adorno's understanding of history as endless disaster actually predates the events of the Holocaust. The remainder of the chapter is devoted to showing how this understanding arises, based on Adorno's response to the intellectual crisis of reason in late nineteenth-century German thought and his perception of the inadequacy of positivist and historicist responses to that crisis (second and third sections). Against this background it becomes possible to discern Adorno's distinctive conception of the task of philosophy (fourth section), and the challenge this poses not only to the Marxist tradition to which his work is most often assimilated by commentators (fifth section) but to contemporary historicism.

Our main source for Adorno's conception of the relationship between philosophy and history is the massive *Negative Dialectics*, a complex and forbidding work which combines criticism of Heidegger, Kant and Hegel with a tentative elaboration of some of the principles of Adorno's own procedure. Useful light is shed on the book as a whole by lectures which Adorno gave while he was writing it, in which these matters are discussed. Of particular value in this context are the lectures on *Metaphysics: Concepts and Problems*. Because much of this material is highly technical philosophical discussion, I have chosen to outline Adorno's method on the basis of his earliest conception of philosophy, in which the stakes are more obvious, and more directly related to categories – nature and culture – which we have already seen in use. In his early essays 'The Actuality of Philosophy' and 'The Idea of Natural History' Adorno is already in possession of much that will characterize his later work, but uses a more approachable vocabulary. Moreover, two essays included in *Critical Models*, 'Progress' and 'On Subject and Object', are useful short guidelines to key elements of Adorno's arguments.

WRITING THE DISASTER

The central difficulty of understanding the relationship between philosophy and history in Adorno's work is that it is easy to see only its negative side. Because Adorno's thought is dialectical – it aims to be always in movement – the points at which it appears to come to rest in what are often memorable aphorisms should not be taken for conclusions. In some ways Adorno's style is his great curse, and his highly condensed formulae can be easily missed as soundbites to be extracted from his texts. Because of their difficulty, knowledge of these gnomic sayings has often substituted for a reading of his works as a whole. The best example of this is the confusion that has greeted

Adorno's comments in his 1953 essay 'Cultural Criticism and Society' that 'to write poetry after Auschwitz is barbaric' (P 34). The reaction of the poet Paul Celan is typical.

Celan is widely celebrated as one of the most distinguished European poets of the post-war period. He was a Jew, and the survivor of a work camp; he had lost both his parents to the Nazis. His work explicitly takes up the challenge of writing poetry after Auschwitz. The strain of the task shows both in the poetry, which is cryptic, fragmentary and sombre, brooding on the limits of language and experience, and in Celan's fragile mental health. Given Adorno's widely publicized comment, and the fact that it was occasionally used against Celan by his critics in the press, some encounter between the two was inevitable. It is unclear quite what Adorno made of Celan's writing, as he never completed an essay on the poet which he is supposed to have planned to write; certainly Celan read Adorno with some care. After Celan failed to turn up to a meeting between the two that had been arranged in Sils Maria, a Swiss mountain town where Nietzsche had spent the summer for a number of years and one of Adorno's favourite places of retreat, instead returning early to Paris, he wrote a prose poem in which Adorno's original surname, Wiesengrund, is encrypted. Adorno's biographer Lorenz Jäger follows John Felstiner's account of Celan's life and work, suggesting that Celan felt an intense ambivalence to Adorno.[3]

Celan is hardly unique in his concern to respond to Adorno's – deliberately – provocative statement. His remarks on the impossibility of writing poetry after Auschwitz have attracted considerable critical scrutiny, and even more notoriety. They appear to cast the Holocaust, for which Auschwitz stands, as an event so traumatic that a direct continuation of the western tradition is impossible: that in a world in which such radical evil is possible, writing poetry would be at best a frivolity, a mere distraction from what Adorno described as a new categorical imperative, the task of ensuring no repetition of such horror would be possible. However, we are in a position to offer a more cautious reading. There are echoes here of issues we have touched on in both the preceding chapters. Remember that the central question of Adorno's aesthetics as a whole is always 'is art possible?', and that his moral philosophy is also posed in terms of the possibility of living a good life in a world which is so radically false. As I have argued, in each case Adorno's intention is not to answer the question, but by posing it in a certain way, to intensify the dialectical tension between culture and barbarism. So Adorno's comments need to be understood as taking their place within his work, considered as an attempt to present negative dialectical thinking in action.

Taken out of context the sentence is possibly worse than meaningless, because it gives such a false impression of Adorno's argument. The preceding lines of the essay make clear that 'the most extreme consciousness of doom threatens to degenerate into idle chatter': the 'dialectic of culture and barbarism' means that even a reflection on or an acknowledgement of the horror of the Holocaust could become a mere passing over, or avoidance (P 34). In other words, not only poetry but any reflection on the Holocaust must encounter the unavoidable risk of becoming complicit in the process of destruction. As Adorno put it later in *Negative Dialectics*, 'All post-Auschwitz culture, including its urgent critique, is garbage' (ND 367). In principle, the statement that lyric poetry is no longer possible after Auschwitz would be as corrupt as that poetry itself. The sentence needs to be read as one half of a tragic dialectic: forget Auschwitz, and participate in the process which sought to erase the victims from history; remember Auschwitz, and risk turning the memory of the victims into a mere gesture, pious and unreflective. Only a way of thinking which takes this double duty into consideration, and absorbs it into its innermost form, would have a chance of not being wholly unjust to the victims of the Holocaust.

The name Auschwitz in particular comes to stand in Adorno's work for the unnameable itself: for the tragedy of history in the face of which transcendental questions about the possibility of philosophy, art and freedom need to be raised. Adorno's attempt to think to extremes runs into difficulties here: by courting the extreme example, his thought risks being caught up in the pathos attached to its name. For a start, it leaves open the misreading which we have seen used against Celan: by naming Auschwitz, a particular event within history, rather than history as such, Adorno appears to ground transcendental enquiry in the empirical realm. But Adorno does not mean that such questions are only needed because of a particular set of events, however horrific. As we have seen in the previous chapters, they are the prerequisites of a genuinely critical enquiry into art and morality in the first place. Secondly, by appearing to treat Auschwitz as an exceptional historical event, Adorno risks reducing its specificity. If Auschwitz becomes a shorthand way of referring to history as such, we have transgressed what we saw in the last chapter as Adorno's sense of the morality of thinking: the negotiation with the violent subsumption of particulars under a concept. If Auschwitz stops being the name for a singular event and becomes identified with history as a whole, the specificity of that event is itself obliterated. Moreover, by being taken into the balance of historical judgement, we accept the horror of the Holocaust into the continuum of normal history. This may succeed in upsetting our sense of normal history, casting it in terms of suffering and domination, rather than the evolution of reason and freedom, but it also risks normalizing and taming catastrophe.

Indeed, Adorno directly anticipates this risk in *Minima Moralia* in a comment on the introduction of the term 'genocide': 'the act of codification that is enshrined in the International Declaration of Human Rights has ensured that the unspeakable has been cut down to size at the very moment that it is protested against'. The 'unspeakable' acts of the Nazis against the Jews have been given a name by international law: the necessary steps to prevent a repetition also efface the singularity of the event, by introducing genocide into the realm of concepts. Adorno's prediction seems horribly accurate, with fifty years of hindsight: 'the day will come when discussions will take place about whether some new monstrous act falls within the definition of genocide'.[4] Adorno's point is not that genocide should not be codified in law, but that there will always be a disjunction between a particular crime and the universality of the law against which it must be judged. The same implacable logic dictates that the unspeakable event of Auschwitz must also be an event like any other. One might argue that the name Auschwitz is already a euphemism, a way to avoid speaking directly of the dead, and of the specific mechanisms of murder to which we understand the word to refer.

Once we understand Adorno's comments as taking their place under the sign of what in the last chapter I called 'the morality of thinking' – in which the very possibility of doing justice to the Holocaust, without simply subsuming it into the logic of equivalence and exchange, is at stake – it becomes harder to view his subsequent reflections on his controversial remarks as retractions rather than clarifications. For example, nearly a decade later, in his 1962 essay on 'Commitment', Adorno both sustains his comment ('I do not want to soften my statement') and acknowledges that the 'rejoinder also remains true, namely that literature must resist precisely this verdict' (NL II 87–8). In *Negative Dialectics* (1966) Adorno appears more contrite: 'perennial suffering has as much right to expression as a tortured man has to scream; hence it may have been wrong to say that after Auschwitz you could no longer write poems' (ND 362). Rehearsing this section of the book in his 1965 lectures on metaphysics, Adorno is more explicit about the misunderstanding of these remarks. His comments 'gave rise to a discussion I did not anticipate', because 'it is in the nature of philosophy . . . that nothing is meant quite literally' (MCP 110). And in 1967: 'The statement that it is not possible to write art after Auschwitz does not hold absolutely, but it is certain that after Auschwitz, because Auschwitz was possible and remains possible for the foreseeable future, light-hearted art is no longer conceivable' (NL II 251). Adorno's restatements are various because no definitive answer is possible: to write or not to write must remain the question.

Note Adorno's phrasing in the last example cited above: it is not merely the future possibility of further planned extermination that threatens the possibility of culture, but the fact that 'Auschwitz *was* possible' (my emphasis). In other words, what the actual historical events of the Holocaust expose is something that had always been a possibility: it is not only the possibility of writing poetry *now* but the possibility of poetry (and ultimately of culture) *itself* which is at stake. This means that Auschwitz cannot function in Adorno's work as the name for the *end* of that history which relates reason, enlightenment, art and morality. In the dark light of the Holocaust the history of the west may look like the road to Auschwitz, but this threatens to disguise the fact that even if the Holocaust had not happened, history would still have been the vehicle of destruction rather than redemption. On the basis of Adorno's account of the morality of thinking, talk about history will always mean the destructive process by which an individual event is subsumed into a more general concept. What concerns us more directly in this chapter is the sense that this destructive process takes place in history as well as in thought: the movement of time is always the obliteration of the past in the name of the present.

In other words, the premise that history is a process of disaster and catastrophe rather than enlightenment comes first in Adorno's work: Auschwitz confirms rather than refutes his understanding of history. Like Walter Benjamin, Adorno rejects narrative history, which can only be an attempt to mask the destructive process of time in an account of the transition from past to present. Strictly speaking, as

Susan Buck-Morss argues, 'Adorno *had* no philosophy of history'.[5] So if, as in *Dialectic of Enlightenment*, Adorno seems to offer a history of enlightenment as disaster, we must remember that this is only the dialectical counter to positive claims made about the progress of reason and the emancipation of humanity. When Adorno writes in *Negative Dialectics* that there is no positive history of human freedom, but that there is a negative history of disaster – 'No universal history leads from savagery to humanitarianism, but there is one leading from the slingshot to the megaton bomb' (ND 320) – he counters a history of spirit with a history of technology. One is not the mirror image of the other: the idea of the progressive development of society is quite distinct from the idea of forms of control by man over nature. So this is not simply a case of standing the Hegelian dialectic of spirit on its head as Marx claimed to have done. Instead there is a hint here at the limits of what history as a discipline can tell us: it can help us catalogue and present the bad news, detailing the forms of domination of man over nature, as Adorno and Horkheimer had done in their joint work. But the question of freedom is simply not a historical one, and requires a critical philosophy to have a chance of emerging. To write a history of culture, as opposed to a natural history in which man is treated as merely another animal, presupposes the possibility of progress. Yet progress is exactly what history itself seems to refute. The solution is that 'universal history must be both construed and denied' (ND 320): as soon as the possibility of progress is assumed directly, progress is betrayed by being turned into another lie in the triumph of domination.

Adorno's presupposition of disaster is not primarily a historical category, but an epistemological and moral one: it is in order to avoid the blind perpetuation of reason's domination over nature that we must reject history. Freedom is always the object of a speculative proposition: just as in previous chapters we have seen Adorno refuse to determine whether or not art or morality are in fact possible, so here we see him deny that history, understood as the progressive emancipation of man through reason, is possible either. This position is clarified in the useful short essay 'Progress', which Adorno describes as a preparatory study for *Negative Dialectics*. Adorno stresses that progress can only mean the progress of mankind as a whole; and only an emancipated humanity would be in a position to discuss progress. Until such a point, progress must remain a speculative proposition. But think dialectically: such an emancipation would also mean that the idea of the 'human' with its implicit division of man from the natural world would itself have to have been dissolved, and perhaps even the idea of progress itself. 'Progress', Adorno argues, 'means: to step out of the magic spell, even out of the spell of progress that is itself nature, in that humanity becomes aware of its own inbred nature and brings to a halt the domination it exacts upon nature and through which domination by nature continues. In this way it could be said that progress occurs where it ends' (CM 150). The 'spell of progress' here links the specific concept of progress to the more general idea of a dialectic of enlightenment: the promise of a release from superstition which drives philosophy is as much part of the problem as it is the solution. Adorno's objective is not so much the perfection of either historical or philosophical enquiry, but the destruction of all the categories with which we think. Pushing arguments to extremes is one of his tactics.

Adorno's materialism dictates that he sees the world as one: truth cannot be relegated to a temporal world beyond history. There is no Christian heaven, no Platonic world of ideals. Only the world of wreckage and disaster surveyed by Walter Benjamin's angel of history: 'one single catastrophe which keeps piling wreckage upon wreckage and hurls it in front of his feet. The angel would like to stay, awaken the dead, and make whole what has been smashed. But a storm is blowing from paradise . . . This storm irresistibly propels him into the future to which his back is turned, while the pile of debris before him grows skyward.'[6] As for Adorno, so for Benjamin, it is this storm which is called 'progress'. In *Minima Moralia* Adorno equates 'the only philosophy which can be responsibly practised in the face of despair' with 'the attempt to contemplate all things as they would present themselves from the standpoint of redemption' (MM 247). For a materialist, redemption could not come from anywhere other than within this world, but as in his analysis of art, where the identification of a work's 'truth-content' will always be a betrayal, so to presume to identify or hail a particular secular redemption would be to abolish its possibility, by proposing both to master history and to curtail the dialectical tension between concepts. It should be clear that in Adorno's eyes this is not resignation, not giving up to disaster, but the only way to engage it without simply perpetuating it. In other words, Adorno's position is not nihilistic, but aims to be the only possible chance of overcoming nihilism. In this he echoes strongly Nietzsche's analysis of late nineteenth-century culture. In the next section I will set Adorno's work into its intellectual context in order to show the specific intellectual currents he sets out to oppose. My broader claim is that these currents have become strong tides, and that for this reason Adorno's obstinacy has more to commend it than ever.

CRISIS OF REASON

Caught between the devastating blow to the nation's confidence of the loss of the 1914–18 war and the accession to power of Adolf Hitler, German culture of the Weimar era was characterized by intense uncertainty and a widespread sense of the need for a radical renewal. Yet it also produced both artists and thinkers who have exerted an enormous influence on the twentieth century. It is sometimes argued that the anxieties of modernity, typical of western intellectuals in the late twentieth century, came early in Germany. Indeed, the very idea of 'modernity' as a sociological phenomenon, alongside many other ideas which we now take for granted, for good or ill, is a German creation. But what needs to be remembered is that the ideas and theories which were to flower in the Weimar period were actually the products of the second half of the nineteenth century. John Burrow sees European thought of that time in terms of a 'crisis of reason', but this was a crisis whose results were already evident before the outbreak of the First World War: 'One thing the war was widely expected to produce was a new cultural epoch. Yet though, as a collective experience, it was far more shattering, more apocalyptic, than could have been imagined, it did not. The extraordinary years 1907–12 had done their work too thoroughly for that.'[7] If the turmoil of the artistic avant-garde predates the conflict itself, we should be wary of ascribing too much influence to the psychological trauma wreaked by first war and then defeat; and in fact the intellectual ferment in which the avant-garde had deep roots was that of the late nineteenth century.

Adorno is a relative latecomer, in other words, to a set of problems which not only dominated the thought of his own time but that remain typical of ours. If Adorno can seem at times like a forerunner of the controversial ideas which emerged from Paris in the 1960s in the work of writers like Michel Foucault and Jacques Derrida, and also speaks to the problems and concerns of the contemporary world, it is because the ways of thinking which he rejects are not those of an ephemeral moment, but underlie what we might think of as a long twentieth century stretching from the 1850s to the present day.

Central to this intellectual turbulence is the encounter between what are now three distinct types of academic discipline, each of which offers a very different model for the pursuit of human understanding: philosophy, history and the natural sciences. For the ancient Greeks philosophy had meant not only logic and metaphysics, but also speculation on the nature of the universe, the collation of current knowledge about the natural world and the study of human behaviour, based in part on the evidence of past events. The last point in European history at which philosophy has been seriously expected to provide such a global view of the world was the early nineteenth century, with the work of Idealist philosophers: Fichte, Schelling and Hegel. But even Idealism felt like a defensive move against the separation of natural science from philosophy in the seventeenth and eighteenth centuries, characteristic of the wider European Enlightenment. By the 1850s philosophy's status as the ultimate arbiter of knowledge was again under threat. The success of the natural sciences in uncovering what seemed to be indisputable laws of nature undermined philosophy, while the immense prestige of German historians of the same period was also built on the attempt to develop a scientific approach to the study of man. The crucial difference between the natural and social sciences was that where the former dealt with laws, the latter sought to understand unique and non-repeatable events. Philosophy, by contrast, withered in the face of the success of these disciplines which seemed so capable of dealing with the laws and facts of the world.

Philosopher and intellectual historian Herbert Schnädelbach describes the development of thought in Germany over this period:

> Nineteenth-century consciousness as a whole achieved its emancipation from Idealism in the name of science and history. In order for this to be possible, the words 'science' and 'history' had to change their meaning, so that they acquired a sense opposite to that which they had, for instance, in Hegel: the change can be expressed in slogan form by saying that now it was 'science *instead of* a philosophical system' and 'historical science *instead of* a philosophy of history'.[8]

Just as over time improvements in the understanding of the workings of the human body lead to medicine and anatomy becoming distinct from philosophy, so in the eighteenth and nineteenth centuries the success of the natural sciences in analysing and explaining the working of the natural world led to an increasingly marked distance between science and philosophy. But once science seemed to have inherited philosophy's claim to speak the truth of the world, philosophy itself began to look rather suspect. Either it was merely irrelevant, since science seemed to offer the prospect of resolving any question put to it, or, worse, it was distinctly suspect: the pursuit of unanswerable questions about the nature of existence or the reality of the world came to look like a remnant of the same superstitions which eighteenth-century philosophy had sought to dispel. But once isolated from philosophy, the same naturalism which we have seen Adorno and Horkheimer deploying to offer a genealogical history of reason becomes a dogmatic and sceptical ideology. Theological or philosophical motifs such as evolution and development were transplanted directly into the study of society and history as a result of their new prestige in the sciences. Exactly the kinds of philosophy of history which Adorno rejects are smuggled back into the human sciences: progress becomes either another myth to be dispelled by the march of reason or a historical assumption.

The rise of the belief that science could offer answers to all those questions that philosophy had traditionally posed, and of a concomitant historicism in the cultural sciences, leads directly to the crisis of reason. On the one hand the determinism of scientific theories of human development reduces the idea of freedom to an illusion. On the other, the human sciences, whose historical investigations were producing an increasing catalogue of different human social practices, seem to lead to a paralysing relativism. From a scientific point of view, philosophical problems of 'truth', 'goodness' and 'beauty' are to be explained away as the index of psychological or physiological impulses. From that of the historians, the description of what people have believed truth, goodness and beauty. to be in different times and places equally fails to provide grounds on which to judge between such beliefs.

Nietzsche is one of the most insightful and influential commentators on this crisis, and his strategies are followed closely by Adorno. In the second of his 'Untimely Meditations' Nietzsche warned against historicism: taken to the extreme, a scientific conception of the world threatens to dissolve man into the flux of the world. Reduced to the epiphenomenon of natural processes, life would be absolutely meaningless: 'a human being who does not possess the power to forget, who is damned to see becoming everywhere; such a human being would no longer believe in his own being, would no longer believe in himself, would see everything flow apart in turbulent particles, and would lose himself in this stream of becoming'.[9] In later works Nietzsche would reverse his position, urging just such an account of reality as purely a process of becoming and transience, judging that humanity needed to be exposed to the ultimate consequences of its system of beliefs in order to destroy those beliefs. The nihilism which Nietzsche sees as endemic in the rise of the natural sciences is to be embraced, as the precursor to a new set of values: only the genealogical destruction of morality will take us beyond good and evil. The key dispute in the interpretation of his work is the extent to which the new values are those urged in his work (a metaphysics of the will recast as a metaphysics of life and vitality, of intensity) or whether these serve only to prepare the way for future values which must remain unspeakable.

Nietzsche was hardly alone in feeling the need for something to fill the gap left by the withdrawal of philosophy and the rise of science, and this is the background to the renewed interest in the work of Immanuel Kant which dominates the intellectual scene around the time of Adorno's birth. Philosophy had been driven back onto its home ground of metaphysics, the study of what is beyond (*meta-*) the natural world (*physis*). Yet 'metaphysical' rapidly acquired the pejorative sense it has today: of a frivolous or unscientific speculation. In this retreat, philosophers lost the critical impulse which had underpinned the work of even the most speculative metaphysicians such as Hegel. The consequence of this are still with us today.

Philosophers realized that, read in a certain light, the work of Kant, a more cautious predecessor of the grandiose metaphysics of Hegel, seemed to provide a more suitably modest model of philosophical enquiry for an anti-metaphysical age. Accordingly philosophy in Germany at the turn of the century was dominated by various schools of neo-Kantianism. With Kant providing a model, questions of knowledge, objectivity and understanding were distinguished from the interpretation of empirical data. While philosophy might refine the models used to understand history, history was itself an autonomous realm of facts, in need of interpretation. The hallmark of neo-Kantianism in all its various forms, was a keen distinction made between the enquiry into objective and timeless laws of logic, and investigation of the empirical world, which could be safely left to other disciplines.

Whereas Kant's own logic was transcendental in seeking to connect the empirical world with the objective categories governing our judgements about what is the case in the world, neo-Kantianism implied a breach between the two. Philosophy was to be concerned with the eternal, with rules whose objectivity could be safely established, away from the messy and chaotic world of historical reality – whose operations could be left to sociology, the new science of society. Philosophy became epistemology, concerned with establishing the objective validity of the methods used by the historical and natural sciences, while its characteristic method became a logic taken to be entirely abstracted from the world whose investigation it sought to govern. As Gillian Rose puts it: 'the three Kantian critical questions "What makes judgements of experience, of morality, of beauty objectively valid?" become the questions "What is the nature of validity in general?" and "What is the relation between validity and its objects?" Logic is separated from cognition, validity from representation, but not from its objects. The result is a general but not a formal logic: a methodology.'[10]

But the inability to connect questions of validity back to the miscellaneous and everyday world was a fatal flaw. With biology, anthropology and sociology threatening to show that the ideas of truth, beauty and right or wrong were merely offshoots of the natural development of the human animal and his social activities, a philosophy which replied by asserting a timeless realm of truth was in a weak position to oppose the rise of a historicism which implied that there was no such thing. In the eyes of Nietzsche and Adorno, the philosophical temptation to separate the real world from the true world, to distinguish an ephemeral and changing world of appearances from a timeless and eternal world of ideals, has now reached its apogee. With the neo-Kantian institutionalization of such a divide, philosophy will never be able to provide answer to the question 'what ought I to do?' because the grounds of morality are either abandoned to science, and therefore to determinism or relativism, or reserved for a higher plane of existence.

By the turn of the twentieth century, philosophy had given up its traditional claims, and seemed to have become the handmaid of science: neither confirming or denying scientific conclusions, but refining and qualifying their grounds. This is what Adorno attacks as positivism: by forgetting that science and philosophy are inventions of man, positivist thought loses the ability to record anything other than *perceptions* of reality, and can never ask about the accuracy or otherwise of these perceptions.[11] This is a characteristic Kantian double-bind: once we acknowledge that the concepts and categories by which we measure the world are not simply out there in the world, but are in some sense frameworks imposed on reality by the mind, how can we avoid solipsism?

Wittgenstein's powerful 1922 statement in the *Tractatus Logico-Philosophicus* of an analytical variant on the neo-Kantian position is typical of much twentieth-century philosophy. He defines the proper territory of philosophy as logic. Only in the realm of logic is there such a thing as necessity or truth. Wittgenstein sketches in dramatic terms the division between the meaningless world of historical accident, and the logical abstractions to which philosophy has access. He attempts to institute a drastic revision of philosophical ambition, which shows most traditional philosophical questioning to be metaphysical and therefore meaningless. He expressly rules out any possibility that philosophy might contribute to concerns such as that of the progress of humanity, or the meaning of history as such. In fact, philosophy's best contribution could be to dissolve these questions entirely, showing them to be meaningless. This is a characteristic positivist account of what philosophy can and cannot achieve. Wittgenstein's resignation in the face of the world runs directly contrary to Adorno's activist sense that, as the product of human labour, society can be changed by man. In this early work Wittgenstein draws a clear distinction between the world as it is, and a world of values; Adorno's materialism insists on a single world, and challenges the notion of value, which grounds metaphysical questions in an economic concept. However, in the desire to heal the world not by further system-building, but by the remedial destruction of incorrect questions, there is a certain amount of common ground between the two men. For all that he sets himself against these philosophical trends, Adorno is just as much a product of his time, as we shall see.

AGAINST HISTORICISM

My central suggestion in this chapter is that Adorno's account of the relationship between philosophy and history can best be seen as an attempt to escape the situation in which neo-Kantianism had mired philosophy. How to reconnect philosophy to the historical world which it had abandoned to the cultural sciences? How to construct a materialist philosophy which does not relapse into the derivation of philosophical questions from supposedly immutable laws of human psychology? How to maintain a critical and transcendental questioning of the validity of knowledge, without closing off the central Nietzschean insistence on history as flux and transformation by insisting on timeless and eternal values? Adorno was far from the only thinker to face this challenge, and the development of his thought as a response to the crisis of reason can best be understood in relation to the work of the preceding generation who had sought to overcome neo-Kantianism, for all of whom philosophy was required to turn back to the things of the world, to accept its place in history.

In fact seeking to reconnect philosophy to human history is one of the most characteristic gestures of twentieth-century thought. In most cases the turn to history has been purely sociological: by accepting the historicist premise that a philosophy must be understood relative to its own historical and cultural context, it has left behind the possibility of critical philosophy. This position presumes a particular understanding of history as a succession of events in time, and certain kinds of connection between thought and its environment: in deriving a philosophy from its context we cannot question the truth or otherwise of the position, which would require the ability to abstract philosophical positions from their historical situations. Equally, such arguments are sceptical, since they rely on a foundation which cannot be called into question within its own terms, but is simply assumed to be true. The choice of history as a ground for the analysis in this case is merely dogmatic.

Those philosophies which have not run into this error, and are not merely revivals of archaic metaphysical positions, derive largely from phenomenology, passing through the work of Heidegger into contemporary French thought, from Sartre to Derrida, on the one hand, and into hermeneutics, represented most famously by Gadamer, on the other. The case of Marxism is more complex, and we will consider it later on. The importance and interest of Adorno's work is that it claims to offer a different path. The chief aim of Adorno's earliest extant philosophical essays is to effect just this negotiation: on the one hand to reject neo-Kantianism, and the separation of philosophy from history; and on the other to keep the phenomenological and hermeneutic tradition at arms-length. Despite his severe criticism of Heidegger, Adorno maintains a distinctive respect for Husserl's work throughout his life, seeing it as the most serious and rigorous renewal of idealism of his age.

In his inaugural lecture at the University of Frankfurt 'The Actuality of Philosophy', delivered in 1931, Adorno confirms that his starting point is rooted in what I have called the crisis of reason: in the failure of neo-Kantianism on one side, and the natural sciences on the other, to connect 'truth' with material 'reality'. Scientific naturalism simply assumes a distinction between subject and object, between nature and the rational science which describes and analyses it. In doing so it can neither give a critical account of its own assumptions, nor give us criteria against which we might evaluate the question of progress, of something more than a merely 'natural' development. From the other side, neo-Kantianism, which equally accepts the exclusion of the natural sciences from the realm of philosophical reflection, has already conceded too much. Positions taken range from a pre-critical (i.e. pre-Kantian) insistence on a realm of timeless value, distinct from nature, to vitalist philosophies which accept the account of natural science but turns one of its categories into a positive value: the intensity of life itself. These positions have complementary faults in Adorno's eyes. The former shields philosophical truth from historical change, but in doing so reduces it to something like a natural law, since it cannot evolve or change. The latter removes the artificial distinction between an ephemeral, fleeting world of appearances and a substantial and eternal world of ideals, but simply erases the possibility of critical thought through the celebration of explicitly irrational values.

The historical turn in neo-Kantianism exemplifies this problem. The historian and philosopher Windelband made a well-known distinction in his lecture 'History and Natural Science' between what he called 'nomothetic' and 'ideographic' sciences: those which find laws (laws of nature for the natural sciences and logical rules for philosophy), and those which are concerned with unrepeatable, singular events. But we might see this as a typical separation of nature from history as realms of enquiry. Bearing in mind our discussion in the previous chapter, it should be clear that this separation must falsify the real dependence of man on the natural world: by treating history as something other than the history of nature, man is turned into something more than an animal. The separation of the natural and historical sciences presumes and is therefore unable to call into question the distinction between history and nature, between man and animal. Under the jurisidiction of neo-Kantian philosophy, the natural sciences construct a deterministic world of natural laws, while history is unable to lift its focus from the empirical historical facts to anything larger. As a result, nature is reduced to an inert material waiting to be shaped by man's activity; on the other hand categories such as freedom and progress are erased from history, which is seen as merely the contingent and accidental array of non-repeatable events.

Adorno takes Husserl's phenomenology as the most important attempt to break out of this neo-Kantian problematic while remaining within philosophical terms. Ultimately, as he argued in his full-length study, Husserl's work remains an epistemology, but what Adorno welcomes in Husserl is his recognition that 'nature' is irreducible to the products of human consciousness. Where neo-Kantianism is happy to see nature as the sum total of all that can be described or analysed within the natural sciences, Husserl underlines that nature is only ever nature *for* a human subject. Philosophy can only be rigorous if it brackets off questions about nature itself, and focuses on the self-critical questioning of our perception, cognition and understanding of the world. Husserl realized that philosophy cannot count itself critical while it depends on grounds external to its scope of questioning. Any attempt to derive understanding from a theory of nature, a theory of history or a theory of psychology must remain sceptical, relying on a theory which cannot be deduced from within its own terms. However, as Husserl himself recognized in his later years, his attempt to refound philosophy, to reestablish a set of first principles on which philosophy might erect itself on a scientific basis, depended on the bracketing off of history. Adorno learns from this failure to be suspicious of any claim to have grounded philosophy on a purely logical basis. If he admires Husserl's rigour, it is because his failure points the way to a central facet of Adorno's philosophical position: that philosophy can never be pure, can never erase its relationship to its objects, which are historical and material.

By this point a range of other thinkers who had recognized the value of Husserl in reinvigorating the idea of a genuinely critical philosophy, but like Adorno had been troubled by the exclusion of history and the material world from the object of philosophical reflection, had sought to blend phenomenology and some form of historicism. Heidegger blends Husserl's work with a sense of history taken from Dilthey. History is to be not the blind spot of phenomenology, but its ground and presupposition. Fundamental ontology posits a common ground for both natural being and historical being.

Man's limited perspective, in which he seems to be set apart from, over and against nature, is outflanked by starting from the assumption of a primordial temporal and spatial flux. Living and thinking become a matter of taking one's bearings in this field of historicity, rather than of uncovering foundations beyond time and space.

Heidegger shares with Adorno a Nietzschean insistence on the primacy of historical transformation and change over eternal or timeless forms. Moreover, by positing history as the ground of phenomenology Heidegger ruins for ever its attempt to become a rigorous science, accepting that there will always be a necessary blindspot in thought, which must always take place in a particular set of historical and social circumstances which it cannot fully reflect on within its own terms. However – perhaps because of this proximity – Adorno marks his distance from Heidegger in emphatic terms. The idea of a fundamental historicity looks to him like a confidence trick. By dissolving both history (that which changes) and nature (that which appears not to) into historicity, change becomes a fundamental principle; but this means dissolving the concretion of history into an abstract principle. Absolute transience might as well be eternal permanence. The process as a whole is elevated above its individual moments: this can be seen as precisely what dialectics, for Adorno, is an attempt to overcome. The concept of mediation means maintaining the tension between the specificity of the moment and its place in the whole, rather than the dissolution of one into the other. This sounds very like Adorno's conception of the value of great music, of course, and the connection is far from accidental.

Here we have something like a basis on which we might develop an account of Adorno's work as a relatively coherent and metaphysical position: a set of assumptions about the ultimate nature of reality from which the philosopher derives a particular way of working. Although I will raise some concerns about whether this is ultimately a valid procedure in regard to Adorno, it is certainly instructive: fracturing the hermetic facia of Adorno's negative philosophy can help us see the fluid, dynamic and open model of dialectics on which much of its positive dimension depends. In *Negative Dialectics* Adorno suggests that 'Bergson's generation – also Simmel, Husserl, and Scheler – yearned in vain for a philosophy receptive to the objects, a philosophy that would substantialize itself' (ND 47). Elsewhere he casts this ambition in terms which are distinctive of the task he and Benjamin had claimed for their own philosophy: 'philosophy's theme would consist of the qualities it downgrades as contingent . . . A matter of urgency to the concept would be what it fails to cover, what its abstractionist mechanism eliminates, what is not already a case of the concept.' Again, Adorno associates this with 'Bergson and Husserl, carriers of philosophical modernism' who 'both have innervated this idea, but withdrawn from it to traditional metaphysics' (ND 8). This provides us with the key to understanding Adorno's ambitions, and the way his philosophy is both an escape from and remains embedded in the characteristic thinking of his early years.

So, to expand on those references to *Negative Dialectics*, Adorno underwrites the concern of the generation before him with a philosophy which would do justice to life itself, to the various and indiscriminate existence of the world, to the diversity and ephemerality of its objects and its lives, and to the independence of things from the consciousness which conceives them. However, he also acknowledges their concern with the way that conceptual thought imposes an abstract schematization on the world, and with the consequent failure of concepts to 'cover' particulars. Conceptual thinking, for Adorno, will never be able to do more than approximate to the world as it is, in its variety and richness: 'no object is wholly known' (ND 14). What the concepts of dialectics and mediation allow for, in Adorno's view, is a conceptual apprehension of the world which acknowledges its own inadequacies, and its own necessary incompletion. But this takes us to the limits of our usual conceptions of philosophy and history. Traditionally philosophy has been concerned with those things which do not change, leaving the changing world to history. Rather than simply reverse this priority as Heidegger does, absorbing change into the premises of philosophy, Adorno turns history into a limit to philosophy, and in doing so hopes to preserve the integrity and autonomy of the particularity of the world, against the absorption of the individual into the whole. Because of its centrality to his concerns, this is a theme which recurs in his work.

In his lectures on *Metaphysics*, which take up precisely the question of the relationship between change and stasis, world and philosophy, Adorno makes a point to which he returns in *Negative Dialectics*, but which can already be seen at work his 1933 essay 'The Idea of Natural History'. Aristotle had understood *physis*, nature, as movement. Hegel had absorbed this into the dialectic, before stabilizing it as a theory of being. But Heidegger's theory 'which seeks to grasp historicity or temporality as an invariant . . . a basic condition of existence' repeats this longstanding philosophical tendency to make 'variability, change itself, into an invariant' (MCP 87). As Adorno puts it in *Negative Dialectics*: 'historicality immobilizes history in the unhistorical realm, heedless of the historical conditions that govern the inner composition and constellation of subject and object' (ND 129). That philosophy which most claims to speak about history as history, as eternal variation and change, in fact turns history back into nature, as the unchanging ground against which man exists. In 'The Idea of Natural History' this criticism becomes a programmatic account of Adorno's own sense of the task of philosophy, which he cites directly in *Negative Dialectics*:

> If the question of the relation of nature and history is to be seriously posed, then it only offers any change of solution if it is possible *to comprehend historical being in its most extreme historical determinacy, where it is most historical, as natural being, or if it were possible to comprehend nature as an historical being where it seems to rest most deeply in itself as nature.* (INH 117, Adorno's italics; c.f. ND 359)

Put more simply, what Adorno wants to argue is that everything which appears to us as natural, everything we take for granted or which seems to be, or to be done, because that's just the way things are, needs to be disenchanted, shown to be the product of a process of becoming. This undoes the authority of that which exists, that which claims to be nothing other than the way of the world: none of this need be the case. But at the same time, nature cannot simply be dissolved into history, which would become an equally 'natural' law, but one of change and transience rather than of stability and permanence: we would simply be replacing the authority of one kind of law with another, historical becoming would overwhelm all the particular moments of history. Marxist critique, into which Adorno's work is often mistakenly assimilated, tends to turn ideas and concepts into historical products. Adorno shares this materialist approach, but takes the next step too, which admits that the idea of history, indeed of materialism, must itself be a historical product. It can never be a fixed and definite ground from which to stake a claim to certainty. Thinking must always be provisional, flexible and risky, exposed to counter-claims and refutation. If history and ideas are historical products, they cannot be used as a basis on which to found a theory, without disregarding their own historical constitution: that they too are shot through with history in their turn, and thus exposed to transformation in the stream of time.

Beneath the negative dialectic seems to lie what can only be described as a metaphysical account of the natural history of the world: both history and nature are fundamentally forms of change and variation. To contrast the history of man against the invariance of nature is to divide man from nature; but to see both man and nature as changing appears to leave no ground on which to judge, for example, freedom. To avoid repeating the idealist metaphysics of Bergson, the world as flux must be seen as destructive rather than creative: as the postponement of reconciliation rather than its achievement. This destruction is manifest in part as the alienation of man from nature, and thus the impossibility of directly conceiving history and nature as co-extensive, which would mean claiming to have ended their alienation. In other words, if Adorno does subscribe to this view of history and nature it cannot become an ontology: it cannot serve as the foundation for a new philosophy. It is not the absorption of history into philosophy or turning of philosophy into history. If for Adorno truth becomes historical, this does not make it the object of a revised kind of philosophical investigation; rather it can only become the object of a historical investigation, at the limit of philosophy. This determines the fact that Adorno's distinctive conception of the task of philosophy is as interpretation and criticism, posing a direct challenge to the idea of philosophy as a system. Philosophy cannot absorb historical particulars, and the confession of such an inability must be such that it cannot drive a new theory, but only become a practice of interpretation.

THE TASK OF PHILOSOPHY

The chapter headed 'Natural Beauty' in the posthumously published *Aesthetic Theory* not only sheds some helpful retrospective light on Adorno's dialectical understanding of the relationship between history and nature, but can illustrate how this is related to Adorno's conception of the task of philosophy as *interpretation*. Since the eighteenth century, the idea of natural beauty has not been particularly influential. Adorno argues that it 'vanished from aesthetics as a result of the burgeoning domination of the concept of freedom and human dignity' (AT 62). The pleasures afforded by art, the product of man, and thus of reason, must be superior to those of mere nature: the progressive development of aesthetics was also an alliance with the domination of reason and history over nature which we have traced in the previous chapters. Art, which raises itself above nature, needs to be judged against its claim to be more than nature: which is why Adorno can seem so severe on the subject. Nor can there be any question of simply turning to nature instead of art: what we perceive to be natural is in reality mediated through society which 'not only provides the schemata of perception but peremptorily determines what nature means through contrast and similarity' (AT 68). The idea of natural beauty, erased in the development of art, returns as a kind of bad faith. Wherever we think we see natural beauty we see only consolatory inversions of our predicament: 'Natural beauty is ideology where it serves to disguise mediatedness as immediacy' (AT 68). Like the leisure industry, which subsumes a parody of freedom within the system of exchange, the tourist industry pre-packages and reduces nature to what Adorno often describes as a nature reserve.

But in addition to a stress on mediation which sees the world in terms of a second nature, Adorno's negative dialectics also implies something like an uncanny return of the repressed. Natural beauty lives on as the bad conscience of art. Indeed Adorno claims that natural beauty is the essential precursor of all beauty in art, and the condition for a 'genuine experience' of art (AT 63). The authentic experience of art would be that of the trace of the world which is obliterated in the construction of the art work, 'the trace of the nonidentical in things under the spell of universal identity' (AT 73). The task of philosophy is the interpretation of second nature to expose it *as* second nature; to uncover the erasure of any 'first' nature. Philosophy cannot claim to restore first nature, indeed this is the point of Adorno's emphasis on mediation and dialectics. But by pointing out the trace of that which has not yet finally been obliterated by man's domination of nature, philosophy attests to a hope of a future transformation. This is a complex figure, however, since that transformation will have to come through the very critical philosophy whose task is being demonstrated.

In his book on Husserl, *Against Epistemology*, the bulk of which was written a few years after his lecture on natural history was given, Adorno describes dialectics as 'the quest to see the new in the old instead of just the old in the new. As it mediates the new, so it also preserves the old in the mediated' (AE 38). In other words, the task of critical philosophy is to intervene in the world and to show that everything which appears to be solid, stable, fixed and immutable, everything which looks as if it is some kind of natural law, is in fact merely the temporary stabilization of unstable forces: to challenge the authority of what appears old by showing that it too was once new. But this is paired with the criticism of the new, by showing that there is no such a thing as a pure escape from the past. More aphoristically, in *Negative Dialectics* Adorno suggests that 'it is when things in being are read as a text of their becoming that idealistic and materialistic dialectics touch' (ND 52).

We are very close to Adorno's idea of 'truth-content' in art, which as we saw in Chapter 2 is something like a singular and unique historical existence at a particular space and time, but which cannot be directly grasped or appreciated. This nominalistic account of truth reflects Adorno's anti-systematic and anti-foundational account of philosophy.

There is another reason why truth must lie in the particular, rather than in the process as a whole, which is that this guarantees the distinction between history and nature: between something which changes, and can be changed, and something which stays the same (even as it develops). For Adorno to salvage some kind of optimism from what would otherwise be a purely deterministic materialism, the account of the perpetual failure of human history to be anything other than a repetition of the violent state of nature usually ascribed to prehistory, he needs to insist on the idea of the new. History depends on the emergence of something quantitatively new, something in addition to the general flux which characterizes existence, and to the return of the archaic: history might still be the product of human labour and self-improvement. History, Adorno comments, is 'characterized primarily by the occurrence of the qualitatively new; it is a movement that does not play itself out in mere identity, mere reproduction of what has always been' (INH 111). If nature is that which appears to be fixed, history is its opposite, becoming. History is the emergence of the new against the background of mere repetition; but history can only be found in the examination of its decayed products which have turned back into nature. Philosophy, or Adorno's understanding of it at least, means the attempt to discern the new in the old, and the old in the new: to trace the inevitable regression, ossification and freezing of the movement of history, and to identify the trace of what was once new in what appears to us as old.

This helps to explain the way in which the distinction between standardized and non-standardized art continues to function in Adorno's work, despite the fact that all art is a suitable subject for criticism. The specific sense of the new in which Adorno is interested can come from autonomous art, but not commodity art. But the arrival of this idea of the 'new', like such terms as freedom and progress, is not assured; rather, the criticism of art will mostly be the assessment of the failure of the new. This explains the curious phenomenon that Adorno's criticism often seems to imply, that such novelty was possible, that art *has* been possible, while being reluctant to point to any successful current art.

Or in terms of the dialectic of enlightenment, we might put it this way. On the one hand, Adorno pursues the Enlightenment procedure of criticizing mythic survivals in the name of reason; on the other, he criticizes the inevitable relapse of enlightenment itself into myth. Adorno and Horkheimer's interest in myth in *Dialectic of Enlightenment* makes this quite plain: they do not simply pit philosophy against myth, but argue that myth emerges as an attempt to rationalize, understand and control the world by accounting for the contingencies and regularities of existence in the face of nature. Just as enlightenment freezes and becomes mythic, myth was already a form of enlightenment. This claim undercuts any account of 'modernity' or 'progress', and much of Adorno's empirical sociological investigation is concerned to demonstrate the survival of pre-rational or non-rational ways of behaving in the people's everyday lives. (Note that this need not be interpreted as an attack on everyday life, merely on any theory which seeks to treat everyday life as normative, or which refuses to allow for the possibility of progress, i.e. for people to hold a more critical relationship to the world.) In his study on the astrology columns of the *LA Times* Adorno sees a desire for people to control their fate by mastering contingency, but also the same manipulation of people's hopes, fears and expectations as displayed in the radio broadcasts of the authoritarian and anti-Semitic preacher Martin Thomas. Adorno sees there, for example, an apparently illogical rhetoric, which is actually the result of highly logical decisions as to how best to exploit people's irrational emotions.

Adorno's reading of Wagner's use of myth in his book *In Search of Wagner* is a particularly condensed example of his interpretative strategies. Note that he is not concerned to simply praise or blame Wagner: he wishes to trace in his work its inescapable historical elements. Wagner's use of myth is intended to be demythologizing: he creates mythic men to replace the idea of the gods, erects secular theologies in order to free man from his supernatural idols. However, the myth of the universal essence of the human undergoes just the sort of petrifaction of which Adorno is most suspicious, and undermines reason – which ought to keep moving as perpetual self-criticism – by becoming stuck. Reason becomes a static property of man, a fixed category, and man is not released from his existence in the world of second nature, a continuation rather than a break from the archaic natural world of violence and the satisfaction of immediate needs, from which society was supposed to represent a break. But this failure of Wagner becomes something like his success for Adorno: by reverting to myth, Wagner's demythologization bears out the schema of the dialectic of enlightenment, and the whole bears out the return of the old (i.e. myth, nature) in the apparently new (art, human). It is not the task of Adorno's critical philosophy to identify how art should or should not be made – that is a dialectic inherent to art itself – but rather to take art as the material for its own critical operation on the world. The results of that operation may be the same every time: a hint of progress, of emancipation, of something different; but the real test of Adorno's work is how convincingly this can be demonstrated from the material it digests, and how rigorously the dialectic of each concept can be seen to be carried through. Philosophy cannot be judged by its fidelity to history, since this assumes the truth of history, but can only be judged by the extent to which it in turn liberates or releases the shock of the new.

It is to avoid the perilous alternatives of a philosophy which has excluded history from its domain, and one which has dissolved history into time, that Adorno's own attempt to establish a critical philosophy of history takes shape. History and nature cannot simply be reduced one to the other: that would imply either a purely formal historicity, or endless repetition, change that was no real change. By understanding the dialectic by which history turns into nature, but by which history emerges in nature, we can treat the whole world as both natural and historical: by showing that what presents itself as natural (whether in the so-called nature or society) is the product of a process of change and becoming, we can underline the potential for further change. But we cannot simply point to the new, only the fossilized forms of the old. Moreover, thinking must acknowledge its own loss of sovereignty. The attempt to admit history into philosophy – or to maintain the tension between the two – must also include the confession of philosophy's own dependence on the non-conceptual.

In *Negative Dialectic* and his later philosophical works, Adorno recasts the argument in epistemological terms. Just as it can be used to form the opposite of culture, society and history, nature can also be used to mean something like the outside world, or the world in general. When Adorno's more overtly philosophical writings, particularly *Against Epistemology* and *Negative Dialectics*, use the distinction between subject and object, they replace the idea of nature with the term 'object'. The subject, that which perceives, acts on or reflects upon the world, is part of that world, is itself an object. But in conceiving itself as perceiving or acting upon the world, it separates itself from it. This situation is Adorno argues 'both real and semblance' (CM 246). It exists, but it need not, and must not be hypostatized, mistakenly assumed to be necessary: we might think of it as historical in having come to be, but therefore exposed to dissolution. However, that dissolution could not be the result of simply thinking of something else: once separation has occurred, there can be no looking back, since the separation was the very constitution of subjectivity, of culture and society. Like the blissful identity between man and nature, that of subject and object is 'romantic', sometimes 'a wishful projection, today just a lie' (CM 246). Non-identity, the overflow of the world from the categories within which thought seeks to immobilize it, cannot just be apprehended or – precisely, the point – identified.

Adorno understands Nature to be tied up with not only the relation between freedom and society, but also the very possibility of a thought which does justice to its object. Indeed, we are now in a better position to characterize Adorno's conception of the task of philosophy as criticism – whether of philosophical movements, of social phenomena, of art, of moral arguments or of historical events. Each is mined, not for some deeper significance or meaning, and certainly not for anything which we might take as evidence of progress towards redemption, but for something more like a non-truth, a bearing witness to the failure of the process of reason, or a stalling of man's emergence to cultured maturity. But the fact of bearing witness and the process of critical thinking both still attest to the promise that there might be more reason and more justice in the world, however attenuated such a prospect might seem under present conditions. History is certainly a fundamental category of Adorno's work: this is why Adorno insists that natural beauty is not ahistorical but historical, and that natural beauty is history at a standstill 'suspended history, a moment of becoming at a standstill' (AT 71). But this is not a new foundationalism. Rather history functions rather more like a negative limit to subjective thought (it runs up against the mobile, everchanging object). As we have seen, becoming functions as something like a historical principle for Adorno, but this becoming is betrayed by identification: a self-reflective and critical reason can only suspend or freeze it, in the hope that this will not channel or determine it. Reason, which makes things exchangeable must not obliterate the trace of the non-identical. The philosophical conceptualization of either the flux of existence or the object which stands against that flux, is as destructive, because objectifying, as the movement of time which sweeps away whatever it creates. This is the disaster, which is neither an ontological nor an epistemological condition, but which appears in thought as a limit or block. Adorno's work can seem at times like a confusing mixture of empirical and transcendental arguments. Certainly, if his doctrine of the primacy of the object is to be taken seriously, this means that Adorno's arguments cannot be confirmed or denied wholly within philosophy, but solely on the grounds of our appeal to and experience of the object, that is of history itself.

His advocacy of the idea of time and history as a destructive flux, within which no redemption is possible is partly an inheritance from his intellectual background, and particularly from Nietzsche: however for Adorno it more clearly functions as a critical tool rather ·than a substantive one. As we have seen he also deploys other historical accounts and genealogies in presenting his positions. But rather than a new philosophy of history, or a new ontology, Adorno treats it as something like a negative principle, a limit up against which thought runs, and a permanent temptation to be resisted. Even if Adorno does inherit the late nineteenth-century attraction to the idea of change and impermanence, he refuses to elevate this into a positive principle. Instead it becomes something like a negative principle, a limit to thought rather than a new foundation. What looks like an ontology of negativity is actually an attempt to resist ontology; what looks like philosophy of history is actually resistance to it.

ADORNO AND MARXISM

The relationship between Adorno and the various traditions of Marxist thought is problematic. The conception of philosophy as criticism which I have outlined in this chapter departs conspicuously from basic tenets shared by even widely divergent interpretations of Marx's thought: the question of the economy is conspicuous largely by its absence; the thesis of the domination of bourgeois culture seems to leave no space for the development of a revolutionary subject of history; and, most importantly, Adorno's apparently negative philosophy of history implies at best scepticism, at worst defeatism, about the possibility of concrete progress. It is not perhaps surprising that from a Marxist point of view Adorno's thought has generally been seen as a massive failure, and a warning about the dangers of irrationalism lurking within the western Marxist tradition – i.e. those strands of Marxism influenced by the work of Georg Lukács – as a whole. Meanwhile, contemporary Anglo-American cultural studies and critical theory, which pays lip-service to orthodox Marxist positions, has inherited much of the Marxist caricature of Adorno, despite sharing many of his reservations. It is true that Adorno was influenced by Lukács in his formative years, yet he rejects almost as much as he learns from him; tracing the relationship between the two will allow us to assess the value of Adorno's work for Marxist thought in general. Marxism has been the most persuasive attempt to join a materialist thought to progressive politics in the twentieth century, and so makes the best point of comparison in attempting to specify the distinctiveness of Adorno's own brand of materialism.

The importance of Lukács is that, as Lucio Colletti comments, *History and Class Consciousness* is the first book 'in which philosophical Marxism ceases to be a cosmological romance and, thus, a surrogate "religion" for the "lower" classes'.[12] Marxist thought in the early years of the twentieth century had encountered the same difficulties as academic philosophy, and faced its own 'crisis of reason'. The rise of scientific naturalist theories of man and of society appealed to many Marxists, who saw an echo of Marx and

Engels's own predilection for natural science. There is a recurrent temptation within Marxist thought to extend the dialectical theory of history – the idea that history progresses through conflicts between different social forces, the resolution of which generates new antagonisms – into a theory of nature as a whole. This has two dangerous consequences from Adorno's point of view. Firstly, historical development comes to be seen as part of a larger natural process: history is reduced to mere nature, abolishing the problem of freedom; or rather, resolving it one-sidedly in favour of determinism. Secondly, the idea of the dialectic – a historical category – is projected onto the natural world. Like the various attempts to grasp history in ontological terms which Adorno rejects, this is sceptical: positing as a true account of the objective world what is in fact a historical and subjective invention of man. Marxism has regularly faced internal crises over what has been derided as 'vulgar' Marxism; what made Lukács's intervention original, and will characterize western Marxism as a whole, is the turn to Hegel.

Marx had himself been influenced by Hegel, and the subsequent rediscovery of early work by the master thinker in which this inspiration was more directly evident than in central texts like *Capital* lent credibility to Lukács's rereading. He argued that for Marxism to become a truly critical science it must acknowledge itself to be a theory of totality. In other words, like Hegel, Lukács insisted that to reconcile the apparent opposition between man and world, history and nature, subject and object, required a perspective from which the whole of history could be surveyed. Whereas for Hegel this perspective presupposed the existence of the absolute, the unity of both world and spirit, for Lukács this perspective demanded the existence of the working class as a revolutionary subject. The antinomies of modern philosophy were neither to be resolved by the completion of the scientific investigation of the material universe, as the naturalists hoped; nor philosophically, by an improved epistemology or ontology, as neo-Kantians and phenomenologists imagined; but only by a social revolution. Lukács's understanding of Hegel offered Marxism a way of countering its tendency towards a pseudo-scientific determinism while vigorously underlining the Leninist emphasis on the party as the vanguard of working-class revolutionary consciousness. The proletariat replaces Hegelian spirit as the self-consciousness of the world; but if the working class cannot overcome bourgeois ideology by itself, the intellectuals must become conscious on its behalf.

This consciousness must be Hegelian, because only speculative dialectical philosophy can reconcile the tensions between the historical sciences and philosophy, between the empirical, material stuff of reality, and the universal. Truth lies neither in the facts, nor in logic, but in the totality of the world understood as a progressive development towards its own transformation.

There are two aspects of Lukács's work which are particularly congenial for Adorno, although this may be more because they express tendencies and prejudices common to both which were already in the air at the time than a matter of a direct debt of the younger to the older man. However, the connection between the two may account not only for Adorno's insistence on his own debt to Hegel, but also the one-sidedness of his reading of Hegel. Firstly, Adorno and Lukács share a reading of the Hegelian dialectic as open-ended and fluid. The ambivalence of Hegel towards the romantic nature philosophy of Schelling is repeated in Lukács and Adorno, both of whom insist on history and reason against the naturalist or vitalist celebration of flux, but imbue their account of history with an emphasis on transformation and destruction which borders on a similar irrationalism. They both stress the material side of the dialectic, although this means slightly different things in each case. For Lukács it means the priority of history over spirit; for Adorno the priority of the object over the subject, and the particular over the whole. Indeed Adorno's emphasis on the primacy of the object can seem at times like nothing more than a dialectical rejoinder to the Hegelian Marxist insistence on the priority of totality.

Despite their difference over the notion of totality, Adorno does seem to follow Lukács in his central concern for the idea of reification, although he may be drawing as much on Lukács's sources for the doctrine in the sociological thinking of Simmel and Weber, and ultimately, like all four men, on Nietzsche. Reification is the central category by which Lukács can account for the ossification of bourgeois consciousness. It justifies both the need for a revolutionary vanguard to help the proletariat shake off its ideological shackles, and the failure of nineteenth-century philosophy to achieve the transformation of the world demanded by the Romantic reaction against Enlightenment. It also – tenuously, in the eyes of more orthodox Marxists – replaces the economic with the cultural as the central category of critical concern. This is the very definition of western Marxist heresy, from the point of view of Soviet Marxism.

Unfortunately, the term reification is used in a different way by almost every writer who uses it, so getting one's bearings on this is difficult. Indeed, it is often simply used as an alternative name for the types of alienation we have seen diagnosed by the Romantic reaction against the Enlightenment.[13] It will not, I suspect, be possible to establish clearly the extent to which Adorno derives his account of reification from Lukács rather than a shared reading of other sources.

For Adorno, the idea of reification links Marx's idea of commodity fetishism – the alienation of the worker from the product of his labour, and the subsequent 'phantasmagoric' pseudo-reality which things acquire – with the Nietzschean polemic against the way that metaphysics freezes and objectifies reality, and against the concept as the abstract subsumption of sensuous particulars. What Adorno calls reification is better expressed in his term 'identity-thinking': the tendency of reason to objectify what it seeks to describe. But it is easy to sympathise with those critics who charge that as a link between 'identity-thinking' and the critique of capitalism in Adorno's work, this is largely rhetorical. Habermas records his amazement at the indiscriminate use to which Adorno put the term: moreover if it is considered the key to his analyses of culture we miss the specificity of Adorno's criticisms of it.

In *Negative Dialectics* Adorno introduces a new reason to be suspicious of the term. Just as he seeks to overthrow the cultural complaints within bourgeois culture which confirm it rather than criticize it, so the concern over reification suggests a fear of the things; but the object, that which is not the subjective position, is what Adorno also seeks to rehabilitate, to reincorporate into thought. He emphasizes that the solution is not to go back: only by perfecting the self-critical reflective philosophy might we reach freedom, rather than looking back to an un-alienated age (ND 374–5). But it signals that one of the positions Adorno needs to fudge is the link between economics and culture. This need not necessarily be considered a weakness in Adorno's work: the broader thrust of his writing is against a totalizing theory of society, so to discover that we cannot simply map economic onto cultural categories is of a piece with his general nominalism; and in his comments on sociological method, Adorno seems concerned to continue to refine and develop theories of capitalism.

Most of the writers who have sought to defend Marxism from Adorno, or Adorno from the attacks of the Marxists, have done so in order to confirm some kind of orthodoxy or party line. This goes as much for the belated advocates of critical theory who tried to construct a theory that never was on the basis of the fragmentary ruins of the Frankfurt School project of the 1930s, as for Adorno and Horkheimer's radicalized opponents on the campuses of the 1960s. Neither seems satisfactory: the problem of the free and autonomous individual lies at the core of Adorno's thought, but freedom and autonomy can only come through an acknowledgement of their very impossibility. Recognition of the dialectical tension between the object and the subject will always frustrate the attempt to establish a party line.

In *Negative Dialectics* Adorno devotes several pages to the attempt to demonstrate that his idea of natural history can already be found in Marx. However, this may not be so much a question of signalling his debt to Marx, as of opening a new way of reading Marx in the light of his own thought. Adorno cites extensively from Albert Schmidt's recently completed study of *The Concept of Nature in Marx* to support his argument. But Schmidt was Adorno's student, and had doubtless approached Marx's texts looking for the kind of material which anticipated his teacher's own work. If the question of who owes what to whom is complex, this is certainly a clear attempt to open a new path for Marxism, based on approaching the writings of Marx as a rich and open text, in which there is plenty of material to support competing interpretations, whose power needs to be judged not in terms of fidelity to an original idea, but in terms of their productiveness for the future. Not, in other words, as the holy book of a pseudo-scientific religious cult.

In his early essay 'On the Actuality of Philosophy' Adorno seems to anticipate a great many of the charges that will be levelled at his work in his lifetime, and continue to be made today, not only by Marxists. He is 'not afraid of the reproach of unfruitful negativity' which will be made at a philosophy of 'radical criticism' (AP 130). Only by overcoming its own affirmative impulses can metaphysics press beyond itself; only 'philosophy which no longer makes the assumption of autonomy, which no longer believes reality itself to be grounded in the *ratio* . . . will stop there where irreducible reality breaks in upon it' (AP 132). Lukács resolves the alienation of nature from history, man from world, subject from object by dissolving theory into praxis, and elevating the promised triumph of the proletariat to the status of the absolute. Adorno refuses to do so, and aims to present his dialectics at a standstill. He holds onto a more affirmative sense of dialectics as open and productive, but without confusing the dialectics of the concept with the existence of reality, which remains partially closed to rational investigation. The tension between philosophy and history cannot be closed within history, so history as disaster will always ruin the triumph of philosophy, just as irreducible reality will always break in on philosophical reflection. The aim of Adorno's thought is to demonstrate the need to appreciate the complexity of this topology.

CONCLUSION

The famous first line of *Negative Dialectics* reads: 'Philosophy, which once seemed obsolete, lives on because the moment to realize it was missed' (ND 3). The difficulty of reading these words exemplifies the persistent and perplexing problems which have shadowed the reception of Adorno's work. The most obvious interpretation is that there was once a moment in which philosophy might have been realized: our chance has been missed, our time is up, and what remains to us, that which we now call philosophy, is but a bare husk of what might have been. However, this is a reading which accords entirely with the historicist logic which I have been concerned to show that Adorno rejects, not merely in passing, but as one of the primary philosophical and political objectives of his thought. In other words, it presumes both that history is simply external to philosophy, and that philosophy is conditioned and limited by history: if we now live in an anti-metaphysical age, as many twentieth-century philosophers have agreed, we must accept the restrictions that history has placed on the aims and objectives of philosophy. The result is philosophies which reconcile themselves to the world as it is, rather than criticizing it.

So we should perhaps bear in mind that Adorno rarely thinks in sentences, but only in paragraphs, and factor in the immediate context of this statement. Indeed, the next sentence, which refers to 'the summary judgement that [philosophy] had merely interpreted the world' makes it clear that Adorno has in mind Marx's well-known remarks in the eleventh thesis on Feuerbach: 'until now philosophy has merely interpreted the world; the point is to change it'.[14] From this it should be clear that what Adorno has in mind when he uses the word philosophy is the possibility of a revolutionary transformation of the world, a possibility which we need by no means understand to be confined to the Marxist tradition, or even the tradition of Kantian critical philosophy. As Stanley Rosen has pointed out, philosophy's quest for truth has always rested on an implied revolutionary impulse to sweep away mere opinion.[15] It makes more sense to think of Adorno as seeking to recover a critical content already present within philosophy than as opposing some kind of new radical theory to philosophy from the outside. The flipside of this is that the philosophies of reconciliation in their contemporary neo-Kantian or analytic form are barely worthy of the name. But as Adorno insists in 'The Actuality of Philosophy' it is not the suppression of theory by praxis for which Marx asks, but the annihilation of the opposition, which will itself come not in theory or praxis but in the total transformation of the world: 'only in the annihilation of the question is the authenticity of philosophic interpretation first successfully proven, and mere thought by itself cannot accomplish this' (AP 129).

So while Adorno's statement may be a reflection on a possible failure of philosophy's critical potential which has always been the case, there may also be some element of reflection on the historical decline of philosophical aspirations to revolutionary transformation. It is certainly clear that he is taking a critical tangent to the Marxist demand for the replacement of theory with praxis, for the substitution of revolutionary action for philosophical reflection. Even if such a position could ever have been justified, Adorno suspects Marx's comments of anachronism and of just the sort of appeal to irrationalism which lingers in late nineteenth-century vitalism, and underpins in some way almost all of the twentieth-century philosophies of authenticity. Just as a philosophy which cannot accept mediation, inauthenticity, or the failure of conceptual thought to do justice to reality, is not the answer, so the call for revolutionary *practice* will lead more often to the suppression of philosophy than its realization. The track record of radical philosophy as a principle of social reconstruction in the twentieth century is poor enough to allow us to confirm Adorno's opening gambit.

Once we put aside any lingering historicism, the question with which *Negative Dialectics* begins becomes not 'when was philosophy's moment missed?' but 'how should we understand philosophy's belatedness?' The failure of philosophy becomes not an endpoint, but a starting point: something more like the attempt to describe the conditions of possibility for critical thought in a world in which thought will never wholly be able to encompass reality, or provide a perfectly pure logical substitute for it. Adorno sees this as a kind of ultra-Kantianism, carrying the epistemological critique of metaphysics and of ontology forward into the realm of philosophy of history. If Kant's work betrays an optimism about the progress of history, cast in terms of the progressive emancipation of a rational humankind from superstition, Adorno's arguments serve to extend the Kantian block to such concepts as progress, and even to the idea of history as a totality. What appears as a scepticism about the possibility of art and freedom is the only position Adorno will allow that will not betray or debase what remains of the hope for actual progress, as opposed to man's increasing technological domination over nature. The rewriting of the story of Enlightenment to cast reason not as both arbiter and vehicle of man's emancipation from nature, but as the single process of man's continued enslavement to nature and his destruction of the world through the domination of reason, is the most violent form of this position, but it subtends all of Adorno's work.

To understand Adorno as asking when, where and how philosophy has failed is already to presume a way of thinking about history that the task of thought must be to put into question. The objective difficulty of tearing our thinking away from historicist presumptions justifies Adorno's strategies, and testifies to the baleful power of historical thinking. If we argue that philosophy *could* have achieved its aims but has failed, we condemn ourselves to a nostalgic re-creation of philosophy, which we confess can no longer be timely or effective: we deny ourselves both philosophy and the possibility of reconciliation.

The most terrifying aspect of Adorno's work is that the disaster which he seemed to have predicted in his early work was apparently confirmed by the triumph of barbarism in Germany in the 1930s and early 1940s. The extent of this incredible inhumanity may have come as a surprise to Adorno, but its place was entirely prepared in his work from the beginning. Adorno had already issued the *diktat* that we think in the face of disaster before he had to do so himself. But once understood as an epistemological rather than a historical condition, we need to acknowledge that the danger can never have passed. If the task of philosophy is to prevent a recurrence of Auschwitz, this is not the result of a particular historical event which has changed the way we think, but was already the task of reason: a process of self-overcoming which would criticize reason's own claim to sovereignty. Only the recognition that the subject is not autonomous, and the reconfiguration of philosophy based on this insight – which could never be a foundational principle – would allow the possibility of something other than the perpetuation of violent domination over nature. If other thinkers have also sensed the need for new ways of thinking about philosophy in the face of disaster, few have been as unflinching as Adorno in acknowledging that this was always already the case, and that disaster is not a catastrophe which befalls reason from outside, but is constitutive of it, and that everything reason promises us is contaminated by the disaster of history.

Adorno closes *Negative Dialectics* with a reiteration of what we have seen described in his epistemological texts as the primacy of the object; in his moral thought as the animal limit to rational morality; and in his aesthetics as the 'truth-content' or historicity of the artwork. This is the need for thought to acknowledge an inescapable surplus of the historical world of things, people and objects over the conceptual resources available for its appropriation. The priority of the object also means an inescapable fracture of the idea of the free autonomous individual which has guided the objectives of philosophy and culture since the eighteenth century. Autonomy is a pervasive illusion which we need to overcome through accepting thought's dependence on those things it assumes itself to have escaped: man's animal nature; reason's own natural history; the pervasiveness of social relations. The self-reflexive critique of reason is for Adorno the inexorable negotiation of thinking with these limits. Where a vulgar Marxism had ascribed the 'dialectic' to nature itself, Adorno's version of materialism begins with the dialectics of the concept. His critical philosophy prevents any simple appeal to history; but the sheer facticity of history, its welter of individual and particular events, resists appropriation by the critical philosophy. This may be a point of resistance, but it is nothing on which we might take a stand, facticity being a conceptualization of what exceeds the concept, the name for something which can be felt only as the interruption of conceptual thought.

In the final section of *Negative Dialectics* Adorno comments that 'it lies in the definition of negative dialectics that it will not come to rest in itself, as if it were total. This is its form of hope' (ND 406). This is no conclusion, merely a reversion to the beginning of the book: another way of talking about the belatedness of philosophy. Philosophy lives on, but its future survival will depend not on its ability to finally establish its authority and mastery over the historical world, as the modern tradition has dreamed, but on its capacity to acknowledge its dependence on that world. Adorno's materialism means rooting thought in an awareness of the suffering bodies on whose frail frames it rests. We cannot let history abolish philosophy, just as we need to protest against the philosophical attempt to abolish history. This is not so much a matter of interference between two concepts, as between the philosophical concept and what remains heterogeneous to it: historical matter.

NOTES

INTRODUCTION

1 Theodor Adorno, *Hegel: Three Studies* trans. Shierry Weber Nicholsen (Cambridge, MA: MIT Press, 1993), 136–7.
2 Leszek Kolakowski, *Main Currents of Marxism*, vol. 3: *The Breakdown* (Oxford: Oxford University Press, 1978), 357; Martin Jay, *Theodor Adorno* (London: Fontana Modern Masters, 1984), 11.

1: AGAINST AUTHENTICITY

1 Georg Lukács, *The Theory of the Novel* trans. Anna Bostock (London: Merlin, 1971), 29.
2 Edward Said, *Representations of the Intellectual* (London: Vintage, 1994), 41.
3 Leo Lowenthal, 'Recollections of Theodor W. Adorno', *Telos* 61 (1984): 159.
4 Jürgen Habermas, 'Theodor Adorno: The Primal History of Subjectivity Gone Wild' in *Philosophical-Political Profiles* trans. Frederick G. Lawrence (Cambridge, MA: MIT Press, 1983), 100.
5 Robert Hullot Kentor, 'Back to Adorno', *Telos* 81 (1989): 11.
6 Quoted in John Abromeit, 'Remembering Adorno', *Radical Philosophy* 124 (2004): 29; Michael Maar, 'Teddy and Tommy: The Masks of *Doctor Faustus*', *New Left Review* 20 (2003): 119.
7 Dagmar Barnouw, *Weimar Intellectuals and the Threat of Modernity* (Bloomington: Indiana University Press, 1988), 123.
8 Lowenthal, 161.
9 Quoted in Peter Gay, *Weimar Culture: The Outsider as Insider* (Harmondsworth: Penguin, 1988), 84.
10 *The Jargon of Authenticity* trans. Knut Tarnowski and Frederic Will (Evanston: Northwestern University Press, 1973), 31.
11 Quoted in Samir Gandesha, 'Leaving Home: On Adorno and Heidegger', in Tom Huhn ed., *The Cambridge Companion to Adorno* (Cambridge: Cambridge University Press, 2004), 104.

12 Harry Liebersohn, *Fate and Utopia in German Sociology, 1870–1923* (Cambridge, MA: MIT Press, 1988), 12.

13 The Frankfurt Institute for Social Research, *Aspects of Sociology* trans. John Viertel (London: Heinemann, 1973), 23.

14 Theodor Adorno, *Kant's Critique of Pure Reason* trans. Rodney Livingstone (Cambridge: Polity, 2001).

15 Quoted in Rolf Wiggerhaus, *The Frankfurt School* trans. Michael Robertson (Cambridge: Polity, 1994), 238.

16 Andrew Rubin, 'The Adorno Files' in Nigel Gibson and Andrew Rubin eds, *Adorno: A Critical Reader* (Oxford: Blackwell, 2002), 172–90 (174).

17 Donald Macrae quoted in David E. Morrison, 'Kultur and Culture: The Case of Theodor W. Adorno and Paul F. Lazarsfeld', *Social Research* 45 (1978): 331–2.

18 Quoted in Morrison, 'Kultur and Culture', 340.

19 Theodor Adorno, 'A Social Critique of Radio Music', *The Kenyon Review* 18 (1996): 229.

20 Peter Uwe Hohendahl, *Prismatic Thought: Theodor W. Adorno* (Lincoln: University of Nebraska Press, 1992), 21.

21 G.W.F. Hegel, *The Philosophy of History* trans. J. Sibree (New York: Dover, 1956), 86.

22 Theodor Adorno, *The Stars Down to Earth and Other Essays on the Irrational in Culture* ed. Stephen Crook (London: Routledge, 1994); Theodor Adorno, *The Psychological Technique of Martin Luther Thomas' Radio Addresses* (Stanford: Stanford University Press, 2000).

23 Theodor Adorno, 'Who's Afraid of the Ivory Tower? A Conversation with Theodor Adorno' trans. Gerhard Richter, *Monatshefte* 94.1 (2002): 18.

24 Agnes Heller, 'The Frankfurt School', in Jeffrey T. Nealon and Caren Irr eds, *Rethinking the Frankfurt School* (Albany: SUNY Press, 2002), 221.

25 Ibid.

26 Jürgen Habermas, *Autonomy and Solidarity: Interviews* ed. Peter Dews (London: Verso, 1986), 98.

27 Max Pensky, 'Beyond the Message in a Bottle: The Other Critical Theory', *Constellations* 10.1 (2003): 139.

28 Henry Pickford, 'Preface' to Theodor Adorno, *Critical Models* (New York: Columbia University Press, 1998), ix.

29 Adorno, 'Ivory Tower', 20.

30 Edward Said, 'Adorno as Lateness Itself', in Gibson and Rubin eds, *Adorno: A Critical Reader*, 198.

31 Lorenz Jäger, *Adorno: A Political Biography* trans. Stewart Spencer (New Haven: Yale University Press, 2004), 193.

2: ART AND CULTURE

1 Quoted in Rolf Wiggerhaus, *The Frankfurt School* trans. Michael Robertson (Cambridge: Polity, 1994), 73.

2 Lorenz Jäger, *Adorno: A Political Biography* trans. Stewart Spencer (New Haven: Yale University Press, 2004), 133.

3 Quoted by Richard Leppert, 'Commentary' in Theodor Adorno, *Essays On Music* (Berkeley: University of California Press, 2002), 230.
4 Theodor Adorno, *Kierkegaard: Construction of the Aesthetic* trans. Robert Hullot-Kentor (Minneapolis: University of Minnesota Press, 1989), 38.
5 Theodor Adorno, letter to Walter Benjamin, 18 March 1936, in Adorno et al., *Aesthetics and Politics* (London: New Left Books, 1977), 123.
6 Walter Benjamin, *Illuminations* ed. Hannah Arendt, trans. Harry Zohn (London: Fontana, 1992), 245, 247.
7 Theodor Adorno, 'Reconciliation Under Duress', in Theodor Adorno et al., *Aesthetics and Politics* (London: New Left Books, 1977), 161.
8 Theodor Adorno, *Introduction to Sociology* trans. Edmund Jephcott (Cambridge: Polity, 2000), 153.
9 Adorno, *Introduction to Sociology*.
10 Norman M. Klein, *Seven Minutes: The Life and Death of the American Animated Cartoon* (London: Verso, 1993), 177.
11 Pierre Bourdieu, *Distinction: A Social Critique of the Judgement of Taste* trans. Richard Nice (London: Routledge, 1984), 1.

3: FREEDOM AND SOCIETY

1 Robert Savage, 'Adorno's Family and Other Animals', *Thesis Eleven* 78 (2004): 110.
2 Lorenz Jäger, *Adorno: A Political Biography* trans. Stewart Spencer (New Haven: Yale University Press, 2004), 107.
3 Norman Malcolm, *Ludwig Wittgenstein: A Memoir, with a Biographical Sketch by Georg von Wright* (Oxford: Oxford University Press, 1962), 26.
4 Siegfried Kracauer, 'The Cult of Distraction: On Berlin's Picture Palaces', trans. Thomas Y. Levin, *New German Critique* 40 (1987): 95.
5 Theodor Adorno, letter to Walter Benjamin, 18 March 1936, in Adorno et al., *Aesthetics and Politics*, 123.
6 Ibid.
7 Theodor Adorno and Hellmut Becker, 'Education for Autonomy' trans. David J. Parent, *Telos* 56 (1983): 109.
8 'An Answer to the Question: What is Enlightenment?' trans. Mary MacGregor, in Immanuel Kant, *Practical Philosophy* (Cambridge: Cambridge University Press, 1996), 17.

4: PHILOSOPHY AND HISTORY

1 Quoted in Rolf Wiggershaus, *The Frankfurt School* trans. Michael Robertson (Cambridge: Polity, 1994).
2 Similar accusations have been made about changes between the 1944 version and the first published version of 1947.
3 Lorenz Jäger, *Adorno: A Political Biography* trans. Stewart Spencer

(New Haven: Yale University Press, 2004); John Felstiner, *Paul Celan: Poet, Survivor, Jew* (New Haven: Yale University Press, 2001).

4 This section was added to the second German edition of *Minima Moralia* and is not included in the English translation. However, it is included in the selections from *Minima Moralia* available in *Can One Live After Auschwitz: A Philosophical Reader* ed. Ralph Teidemann (Stanford: Stanford University Press, 2003), 60.

5 Susan Buck-Morss, *The Origin of Negative Dialectics* (Hassocks: Harvester, 1977), 49.

6 'Theses on the Philosophy of History', *Illuminations* trans. Harry Zohn, ed. Hannah Arendt (London: Fontana, 1992), 249.

7 John Burrow, *The Crisis of Reason: European Thought 1848–1918* (New Haven: Yale University Press, 2000), 252.

8 Herbert Schnädelbach, *Philosophy in Germany: 1831–1933* trans. Eric Matthew (Cambridge: Cambridge University Press, 1984), 33.

9 Friedrich Nietzsche, 'On the Utility and Liability of History for Life', in *Unfashionable Observations* trans. Richard T. Gray (Stanford: Stanford University Press, 1995), 89.

10 Gillian Rose, *Hegel Contra Sociology* (London: Athlone, 1981), 8.

11 'Sociology and Empirical Research', in Theodor Adorno et al., *The Positivist Dispute in German Sociology* trans. Glyn Adey and David Frisby (London: Heinemann, 1976).

12 Lucio Colletti, *Marxism and Hegel* trans. Lawrence Garner (London: New Left Books, 1973) 178.

13 For a detailed discussion of theories of reification see Gillian Rose, *Melancholy Science: An Introduction to the Thought of Theodor W. Adorno* (London: Macmillan, 1978).

14 Karl Marx, 'Theses on Feuerbach' in *The German Ideology* (Amherst: Prometheus, 1998), 571.

15 Stanley Rosen, 'Philosophy and Revolution', in *The Quarrel Between Poetry and Philosophy: Studies in Ancient Thought* (New York: Routledge, 1988), 27–55.

FURTHER READING

WORKS BY ADORNO

Adorno's major works are all available in English translation. Of these *Minima Moralia* is probably the best starting point for someone new to Adorno's work, as it demonstrates clearly both the breadth and style of his work. Despite its size, *Aesthetic Theory* is not as unapproachable as one might think. Begin with the draft introduction, and then dip into sections which look interesting. Because of the particular form of the text, a close reading of any one section should give you a strong idea of the argument of the whole. *Negative Dialectics* is probably not for the faint-hearted, and certainly not accessible to those with no interest in philosophy. *Dialectic of Enlightenment* is certainly an easier, but in my view less successful, work. It is currently available in two translations: the Stanford University Press edition is preferable to the Verso, but the latter is not particularly inadequate.

Adorno's various collections of essays provide a good starting point, particularly if your interests lie in the cultural criticism more than the philosophical side of his work. *Critical Models* is highly recommended, and would make a good introduction to Adorno's work, as many of the essays were written for radio broadcasts and so are relatively approachable. Richard Leppert's collection *Essays on Music* is a hugely impressive book, with an excellent selection of texts by Adorno with comprehensive and astute editorial material. *Prisms* was the first of Adorno's books to be translated into English, and contains the helpful 'Cultural Criticism and Society': however, the value of the other essays in the volume may depend on your familiarity with their subject matter (Spengler, Veblen, etc.). For those with a literary background, the two volumes of *Notes on Literature* will be of interest, particularly Adorno's essays 'Lyric Poetry and Society' and on Beckett's *Endgame* in Volume 1. 'The Essay As Form' which begins that volume may make a useful introduction to Adorno's ideas about his own style of writing. There are two readers available of texts by Adorno. *Can One Live After Auschwitz? A Philosophical Reader*, edited by Rolf Tiedemann, is an excellent selection, containing extracts from *Minima Moralia* as well as essays from all areas of Adorno's oeuvre, and concluding with a helpful selection from Adorno's lectures on *Metaphysics*. The *Adorno Reader*, edited by Brian O'Connor, is less helpful, but reprints some hard-to-find essays, so is certainly worth a look.

SECONDARY READING

General

The best introduction to Adorno's work currently in print is Simon Jarvis's *Adorno: A Critical Introduction*. If you are looking for a more detailed and thorough account of Adorno's thought, it should certainly be your next step. Gillian Rose's *The Melancholy Science: An Introduction to the Thought of Theodor W. Adorno* is also an excellent, although possibly harder, work. It is out of print, but worth tracking down. Susan Buck-Morss's *The Origin of Negative Dialectics* is very thorough, although it only covers the early years of Adorno's career. Hauke Brunhorst's *Adorno and Critical Theory* is informative and approachable, stressing the philosophical rather than the aesthetic side of Adorno's work. Although it is not explicitly an introductory text, Shierry Nicholson Weber's *Exact Imagination, Late Work: On Adorno's Aesthetics* is exemplary for its attention to detail. It is particularly helpful as an example of how to read Adorno with the same care that he put into the construction of his work. Thomas Pepper's essay 'Guilt by (un)free association' is also a breathtaking demonstration of how Adorno might be read. For biographical and background information Rolf Wiggershaus's *The Frankfurt School: Its Histories, Theories and Political Significance* is the standard history, having superseded Martin Jay's *The Dialectical Imagination: A History of the Frankfurt School and the Institute of Social Research, 1923–50*. Lorenz Jäger's recently published *Adorno: A Political Biography* adds some detail, but is not an accurate guide to Adorno's thought. Translations of fuller biographies by Detlev Claussen and

Stefan Muller-Doohm are forthcoming. Many of the essays in *The Cambridge Companion to Adorno: Adorno A Critical Reader* and *A Handbook of Critical Theory* are also helpful.

Aesthetics

Adorno's work on aesthetics has been subject to the most extensive discussion and the reader is well-served for books on this topic. Shierry Weber Nicholson's excellent *Exact Imagination, Late Work: On Adorno's Aesthetics* has already been mentioned. The collection of essays entitled *The Semblance of Subjectivity* is very good, and because of its breadth would make a decent introduction to Adorno's work as a whole. Lambert Zuidervaart's *Adorno's Aesthetic Theory: The Redemption of Illusion* is a useful introduction, while Christoph Menke's *The Sovereignty of Art: Aesthetic Negativity in Adorno and Derrida* is more complex. On the question of Adorno's writing on popular culture, Deborah Cook's *The Culture Industry Revisited* is a sophisticated survey, Robert Witkin's *Adorno on Popular Culture* bright and breezy.

Moral Philosophy

Adorno's contribution to moral thought has only recently begun to be addressed in English-language work. This makes the essays by Christoph Menke and Gerhard Schweppenhäuser in *The Cambridge Companion to Adorno* essential reading. J.M. Bernstein's *Adorno: Disenchantment and Ethics* is a massive examination of Adorno's relevance to contemporary debates in moral philosophy, but probably not the best starting point for the beginner.

Philosophy and History

Brian O'Connor's *Adorno's Negative Dialectic: Philosophy and the Possibility of Critical Rationality* is an important work which seeks to give a relatively systematic account of Adorno's relation to philosophers such as Kant, Hegel, Husserl and Heidegger. The first half of Alex Garcia Düttmann's *The Memory of Thought: An Essay on Adorno and Heidegger* is a powerful and sympathetic meditation on Adorno's thought. Fredric Jameson's *Late Marxism: Adorno, or, The Persistence of the Dialectic* is an ambitious but controversial attempt to assess the timeliness of Adorno. More specialist studies include Eric L. Krakauer's *The Disposition of the Subject: Reading Adorno's Dialectic of Technology*, Karin Bauer's *Adorno's Nietzschean*

Narratives: Critiques of Ideology, Readings of Wagner. Steven Vogel's *Against Nature: The Concept of Nature in Critical Theory* and Anson Rabinach's *In the Shadow of Catastrophe: German Intellectuals Between Apocalypse and Enlightenment* are broader studies which give important insights into the intellectual background to Adorno's thought. Michael Rosen's *Hegel's Dialectic and Its Criticism* contains a significant assessment of the links between Adorno's and Hegel's ideas of the dialectic.

BIBLIOGRAPHY

The bibliographies of works by and about Adorno are not comprehensive. A recent extensive bibliography is available in *The Cambridge Companion to Adorno*, ed. Tom Huhn.

WORKS BY ADORNO

Adorno *et al.*, *Aesthetics and Politics* London: New Left Books, 1977.
'The Actuality of Philosophy', *Telos* 31 (1977): 120–33.
Aesthetic Theory trans. Robert Hullot-Kentor, London: Athlone, 1992.
Against Epistemology: A Metacritique trans. Willis Domingo, Oxford: Blackwell, 1982.
Can One Live After Auschwitz? A Philosophical Reader ed. Ralph Teidemann, trans. Rodney Livingstone *et al.*, Stanford: Stanford University Press, 2003.
Composing for the Films with Hans Eisler, London: Athlone Press, 1994.
Critical Models trans. Henry Pickford, New York: Columbia University Press, 1998.
The Culture Industry: Selected Essays on Mass Culture ed. J.M. Bernstein, London: Routledge, 1991.
Dialectic of Enlightenment: Philosophical Fragments with Max Horkheimer, trans. Edmund Jephcott, Stanford: Stanford University Press, 2002.
Dialectic of Enlightenment with Max Horkheimer, trans. John Cumming, London: New Left Books, 1972.
'Education for Autonomy', Theodor Adorno and Hellmut Becker, trans. David J. Parent, *Telos* 56 (1983): 103–10.
Essays on Music ed. Richard Leppert, Berkeley: University of California Press, 2002.
Hegel: Three Studies trans. Shierry Weber Nicholsen, Cambridge, MA: MIT Press, 1993.
'The Idea of Natural History', trans. Robert Hullot-Kentor, *Telos* 32 (1977): 111–24.
In Search of Wagner trans. Rodney Livingstone, London: Verso, 1981.
Introduction to Sociology trans. Edmund Jephcott, Cambridge: Polity, 2000.

The Jargon of Authenticity trans. Knut Tarnowski and Frederic Will, Evanston: Northwestern University Press, 1973.

Kant's 'Critique of Pure Reason' trans. Rodney Livingstone, Cambridge: Polity, 2001.

Kierkegaard: Construction of the Aesthetic trans. Robert Hullot-Kentor, Minneapolis: University of Minnesota Press, 1989.

Metaphysics: Concepts and Problems trans. Edmund Jephcott, Cambridge: Polity, 2000.

Minima Moralia trans. Edmund Jephcott, London: New Left Books, 1974.

Negative Dialectics trans. E.B. Ashton, London: Routledge, 1973.

Notes to Literature 2 vols. trans. Shierry Weber Nicholsen, New York: Columbia University Press, 1991, 1992.

Philosophy of Modern Music trans. Anne G. Mitchell & Wesley V. Blomster, London: Continuum, 2003.

The Positivist Dispute in German Sociology trans. Glyn Adey and David Frisby, London: Heinemann, 1976.

Prisms trans. Samuel and Shierry Weber, Cambridge, MA: MIT Press, 1981.

Problems of Moral Philosophy trans. Rodney Livingstone, Cambridge: Polity, 2000.

The Psychological Technique of Martin Luther Thomas' Radio Addresses Stanford: Stanford University Press, 2000.

Quasi Una Fantasia: Essays in Modern Music trans. Rodney Livingstone, London: Verso, 1992.

'A Social Critique of Radio Music', *The Kenyon Review* 18 (1996): 229–35.

Sound Figures trans. Rodney Livingstone, Stanford: Stanford University Press, 1999.

The Stars Down to Earth and Other Essays on the Irrational in Culture ed. Stephen Crook, London: Routledge, 1994.

'Theory of Pseudo-Culture', trans. Deborah Cook, *Telos* 95 (1993): 15–38.

'Who's Afraid of the Ivory Tower? A Conversation with Theodor Adorno' trans. Gerhard Richter, *Monatshefte* 94.1 (2002): 10–23.

SECONDARY WORKS ON ADORNO

Abromeit, John 'Remembering Adorno', *Radical Philosophy* 124 (March/April 2004): 27–38.

Bauer, Karin *Adorno's Nietzschean Narratives: Critiques of Ideology, Readings of Wagner* Albany: SUNY Press, 1999.

Bernstein, J.M. *Adorno: Disenchantment and Ethics* Cambridge: Cambridge University Press, 2001.

Brunkhorst, Hauke *Adorno and Critical Theory* Cardiff: University of Wales Press, 1999.

Buck-Morss, Susan *The Origin of Negative Dialectics* Brighton: Harvester Press, 1977.

Cook, Deborah *The Culture Industry Revisited: Theodor W. Adorno on Mass Culture* Lanham, MD: Rowman & Littlefield, 1996.

Düttmann, Alexander Garcia *The Memory of Thought: An Essay on Heidegger and Adorno* trans. Nicholas Walker. London: Athlone, 2002.

Gibson, Nigel and Rubin, Andrew *Adorno: A Critical Reader* Oxford: Blackwell, 2002.

Habermas, Jurgen 'Theodor Adorno: The Primal History of Subjectivity Gone Wild', in *Philosophical-Political Profiles* Cambridge, MA: MIT Press, 1983.

Hohendahl, Peter Uwe *Prismatic Thought: Theodor W. Adorno* Lincoln: University of Nebraska Press, 1992.

Huhn, Tom (ed.) *The Cambridge Companion to Adorno* Cambridge: Cambridge University Press, 2004.

Huhn, Tom & Zuidervaart, Lambert (eds) *The Semblance of Subjectivity: Adorno's Aesthetic Theory* Cambridge, MA: MIT Press, 1997.

Hullot Kentor, Robert 'Back to Adorno', *Telos* 81 (1989): 5–29.

Jäger, Lorenz *Adorno: A Political Biography* trans. Stewart Spencer, New Haven: Yale University Press, 2004.

Jameson, Frederic *Late Marxism: Adorno, or, The Persistence of the Dialectic* London: Verso, 1990.

Jarvis, Simon *Adorno: A Critical Introduction* Cambridge: Polity, 1998.

Jay, Martin *The Dialectical Imagination: A History of the Frankfurt School and the Institute of Social Research, 1923–50* Berkeley: University of California Press, 1973.

—— *Adorno* London: Fontana, 1984.

Krakauer, Eric L. *The Disposition of the Subject: Reading Adorno's Dialectic of Technology* Evanston: Northwestern University Press, 1998.

Lowenthal, Leo 'Recollections of Theodor W. Adorno', *Telos* 61 (1984): 158–65.

Maar, Michael 'Teddy and Tommy: The Masks of *Doctor Faustus*', *New Left Review* 20 (2003): 113–30.

Menke, Christoph *The Sovereignty of Art: Aesthetic Negativity in Adorno and Derrida* trans. Neil Solomon, Cambridge, MA: MIT Press, 1998.

Morrison, David E. 'Kultur and Culture: The Case of Theodor W. Adorno and Paul Lazarsfeld', *Social Research* 48.2 (1978): 331–55.

Nicholson, Sherry Weber *Exact Imagination, Late Work: On Adorno's Aesthetics* Cambridge, MA: MIT Press, 1997.

O'Connor, Brian *Adorno's Negative Dialectic: Philosophy and the Possibility of Critical Rationality* Cambridge, MA: MIT Press, 2004.

Pensky, Max 'Beyond the Message in a Bottle: The Other Critical Theory', *Constellations* 10.1 (2003): 135–44.

Pepper, Thomas 'Guilt by (Un)Free Association: Adorno on Romance *et al.*, with Some Reference to the Schlock Experience', in *Singularities: Extremes of Theory in the Twentieth Century* Cambridge: Cambridge University Press, 1997. Also available in *Modern Language Notes* 109 (1994): 913–37.

Rose, Gillian *The Melancholy Science: An Introduction to the Thought of Theodor W. Adorno* London: Macmillan, 1978.

Said, Edward 'Adorno as Lateness Itself', in Nigel Gibson and Andrew Rubin eds *Adorno: A Critical Reader* Oxford: Blackwell, 2002.

Savage, Robert 'Adorno's Family and Other Animals', *Thesis Eleven* 78 (2004): 102–12.

Vogel, Stephen *Against Nature: The Concept of Nature in Critical Theory* New York: SUNY Press, 1996.

Wiggershaus, Rolf *The Frankfurt School: Its History, Theories and Political Significance* trans. Michael Robertson, Cambridge: Polity, 1994.

Witkin, Robert *Adorno and Popular Music* London: Routledge, 2003.

Zuidervaart, Lambert *Adorno's Aesthetic Theory: The Redemption of Illusion* Cambridge, MA: MIT Press, 1991.

OTHER WORKS

Barnouw, Dagmar *Weimar Intellectuals and the Threat of Modernity* Bloomington: Indiana University Press, 1988.

Benjamin, Walter 'Theses on the Philosophy of History', in *Illuminations* trans. Harry Zohn, ed. Hannah Arendt, London: Fontana, 1992.

Bourdieu, Pierre *Distinction: A Social Critique of the Judgement of Taste* trans. Richard Nice, London: Routledge, 1984.

Bürger, Peter *Theory of the Avant-Garde* trans. Michael Shaw, Minnesota: University of Massachusetts Press, 1984.

Burrow, John *The Crisis of Reason: European Thought, 1848-1914* New Haven: Yale University Press, 2000.

Colletti, Lucio *Marxism and Hegel* trans. Lawrence Garner, London: New Left Books, 1973.

Dickens, Charles *Great Expectations* Harmondsworth: Penguin, 2003.

Gay, Peter *Weimar Culture: The Outsider as Insider* Harmondsworth: Penguin, 1988.

Habermas, Jurgen *Autonomy and Solidarity: Interviews* ed. Peter Dews London: Verso, 1986.

—— *The Philosophical Discourse of Modernity* trans. Frederick Lawrence, Cambridge: Polity, 1987.

Hegel, G.W.F. *The Philosophy of History* trans. J. Sibree, New York: Dover, 1956.

Heller, Agnes 'The Frankfurt School', in Jeffrey T. Nealon and Caren Irr (eds) *Rethinking The Frankfurt School* Albany: SUNY Press, 2002.

Ibsen, Henrik *The Wild Duck* in *Hedda Gabler and Other Plays* trans. Una Ellis-Fermor, Harmondsworth: Penguin, 1961.

Kant, Immanuel 'An Answer to the Question: What is Enlightenment?', *Practical Philosophy* trans. and ed. Mary J. Gregor, Cambridge: Cambridge University Press, 1996, 11–22.

Klein, Norman M. *Seven Minutes: The Life and Death of the American Animated Cartoon* London: Verso, 1993.

Kolakowski, Leszek *Main Currents of Marxism* vol. 3: *The Breakdown* Oxford: Oxford University Press, 1978.

Kracauer, Siegfried *The Mass Ornament: Weimar Essays* ed. and trans. Thomas Levin, Cambridge, MA: Harvard University Press, 1995.

Kracauer, Siegfried 'The Cult of Distraction: On Berlin's Picture Palaces' trans. Thomas Y. Levin, *New German Critique* 40 (Winter 1987): 90–6.

Lukács, Georg *The Theory of the Novel* trans. Anna Bostock, London: Merlin, 1971.

Lukács, Georg *History and Class Consciousness* trans. Rodney Livingstone, London: Merlin Press, 1971.

MacIntyre, Alastair *After Virtue* London: Duckworth, 1985.

Malcolm, Malcolm *Ludwig Wittgenstein: A Memoir, with a Biographical Sketch by Georg von Wright* Oxford: Oxford University Press, 1962.

Mann, Thomas *Doctor Faustus* trans. H.T. Lowe-Porter, Harmondsworth: Penguin, 1968.

Nietzsche, Friedrich *On the Genealogy of Morality* ed. Keith Ansell-Pearson, trans. Carol Diethe, Cambridge: Cambridge University Press, 1994.

—— 'On the Utility and Liability of History for Life', in *Unfashionable Observations* trans. Richard T. Gray, Stanford: Stanford University Press, 1995.

Rabinach, Anson *In the Shadow of Catastrophe: German Intellectuals Between Apocalypse and Enlightenment* Berkeley: University of California Press, 1997.

Rasmussen, David M. (ed.) *The Handbook of Critical Theory* Oxford: Blackwell, 1999.

Rose, Gillian *Hegel Contra Sociology* London: Athlone, 1981.

Rosen, Michael *Hegel's Dialectic and Its Criticism* Cambridge: Cambridge University Press, 1982.

Rosen, Stanley *The Quarrel Between Poetry and Philosophy: Studies in Ancient Thought* New York: Routledge, 1988.

Rush, Fred (ed.) *The Cambridge Companion to Critical Theory* Cambridge: Cambridge University Press, 2004.

Said, Edward *Representations of the Intellectual* London: Vintage, 1994.

Schmidt, Alfred *The Concept of Nature in Marx* trans. Ben Fowkes, London: New Left Books, 1971.

Schnädelbach, Herbert *Philosophy in Germany: 1831–1933* trans. Eric Matthews, Cambridge: Cambridge University Press, 1984.

Vogel, Steven *Against Nature: The Concept of Nature in Critical Theory* Albany: SUNY Press, 1996.

Windelband, Wilhelm 'History and Natural Science' trans. Guy Oakes, *History and Theory* 19 (1980): 169–85.

Wittgenstein, Ludwig *Tractatus Logico-Philosophicus* trans. D.F. Pears and B.F. McGuinness, London: Routledge, 1961.

INDEX

Lightning Source UK Ltd.
Milton Keynes UK
UKOW04f1032110813

215146UK00007B/66/P